C-4659   CAREER EXAMINATION SERIES

This is your
PASSBOOK for...

Public Works Supervisor

Test Preparation Study Guide
Questions & Answers

COPYRIGHT NOTICE

This book is SOLELY intended for, is sold ONLY to, and its use is RESTRICTED to individual, bona fide applicants or candidates who qualify by virtue of having seriously filed applications for appropriate license, certificate, professional and/or promotional advancement, higher school matriculation, scholarship, or other legitimate requirements of education and/or governmental authorities.

This book is NOT intended for use, class instruction, tutoring, training, duplication, copying, reprinting, excerption, or adaptation, etc., by:

1) Other publishers
2) Proprietors and/or Instructors of "Coaching" and/or Preparatory Courses
3) Personnel and/or Training Divisions of commercial, industrial, and governmental organizations
4) Schools, colleges, or universities and/or their departments and staffs, including teachers and other personnel
5) Testing Agencies or Bureaus
6) Study groups which seek by the purchase of a single volume to copy and/or duplicate and/or adapt this material for use by the group as a whole without having purchased individual volumes for each of the members of the group
7) Et al.

Such persons would be in violation of appropriate Federal and State statutes.

PROVISION OF LICENSING AGREEMENTS – Recognized educational, commercial, industrial, and governmental institutions and organizations, and others legitimately engaged in educational pursuits, including training, testing, and measurement activities, may address request for a licensing agreement to the copyright owners, who will determine whether, and under what conditions, including fees and charges, the materials in this book may be used them. In other words, a licensing facility exists for the legitimate use of the material in this book on other than an individual basis. However, it is asseverated and affirmed here that the material in this book CANNOT be used without the receipt of the express permission of such a licensing agreement from the Publishers. Inquiries re licensing should be addressed to the company, attention rights and permissions department.

All rights reserved, including the right of reproduction in whole or in part, in any form or by any means, electronic or mechanical, including photocopying, recording, or by any information storage and retrieval system, without permission in writing from the Publisher.

Copyright © 2024 by
National Learning Corporation

212 Michael Drive, Syosset, NY 11791
(516) 921-8888 • www.passbooks.com
E-mail: info@passbooks.com

PUBLISHED IN THE UNITED STATES OF AMERICA

PASSBOOK® SERIES

THE *PASSBOOK® SERIES* has been created to prepare applicants and candidates for the ultimate academic battlefield – the examination room.

At some time in our lives, each and every one of us may be required to take an examination – for validation, matriculation, admission, qualification, registration, certification, or licensure.

Based on the assumption that every applicant or candidate has met the basic formal educational standards, has taken the required number of courses, and read the necessary texts, the *PASSBOOK® SERIES* furnishes the one special preparation which may assure passing with confidence, instead of failing with insecurity. Examination questions – together with answers – are furnished as the basic vehicle for study so that the mysteries of the examination and its compounding difficulties may be eliminated or diminished by a sure method.

This book is meant to help you pass your examination provided that you qualify and are serious in your objective.

The entire field is reviewed through the huge store of content information which is succinctly presented through a provocative and challenging approach – the question-and-answer method.

A climate of success is established by furnishing the correct answers at the end of each test.

You soon learn to recognize types of questions, forms of questions, and patterns of questioning. You may even begin to anticipate expected outcomes.

You perceive that many questions are repeated or adapted so that you can gain acute insights, which may enable you to score many sure points.

You learn how to confront new questions, or types of questions, and to attack them confidently and work out the correct answers.

You note objectives and emphases, and recognize pitfalls and dangers, so that you may make positive educational adjustments.

Moreover, you are kept fully informed in relation to new concepts, methods, practices, and directions in the field.

You discover that you are actually taking the examination all the time: you are preparing for the examination by "taking" an examination, not by reading extraneous and/or supererogatory textbooks.

In short, this PASSBOOK®, used directedly, should be an important factor in helping you to pass your test.

PUBLIC WORKS SUPERVISOR

DUTIES:

Supervises the cleaning, construction and repair of storm and sanitary wastewater lines and catch basins; patching, resurfacing and cleaning of streets, the replacement of curbing and the repair of sidewalks; snow removal and ice control activities on streets, sidewalks, and parking areas; supervises the maintenance and repair of parks and recreation areas; supervises the maintenance and construction of traffic and street signs, the marking of streets and the maintenance of traffic signals and fire alarm boxes; instructs subordinates in the operation of equipment such as trucks, rollers, sweepers, backhoes and other equipment, and in proper methods of performing tasks; assigns and schedules crews to specific tasks; occasionally performs skilled mechanical or construction tasks; assists the superintendent in the planning of bureau activities, and assumes the duties of the superintendent in his absence; maintains a variety of activity and personnel records, and submits oral and written reports; schedules and supervises the maintenance and repair of public-works equipment; recommends hiring, firing, and other personnel actions.

SUBJECT OF EXAMINATION:
The written test is designed to evaluate knowledge, skills and/or abilities in the following areas:
1. **Administrative supervision** -These questions test for knowledge of the principles and practices involved in directing the activities of a large subordinate staff, including subordinate supervisors. Questions relate to the personal interactions between an upper level supervisor and his/her subordinate supervisors in the accomplishment of objectives. These questions cover such areas as assigning work to and coordinating the activities of several units, establishing and guiding staff development programs, evaluating the performance of subordinate supervisors, and maintaining relationships with other organizational sections.
2. **Maintenance and reconstruction of streets, sidewalks and curbs** -These questions test for knowledge of the proper methods, materials and equipment used in the installation, repair and upkeep of street surfaces, utility access holes, gutters, catch basins, curbing and sidewalks, including ice and snow removal and control.
3. **Maintenance and construction of sanitary and storm sewer systems** -These questions test for knowledge of the proper methods, materials and equipment used in the installation, maintenance, repair and cleaning of sanitary and storm sewers, catch basins and related appurtenances; and proper trenching and backfilling procedures.
4. **Safety practices** -These questions test for knowledge of and the ability to apply safety principles related to construction and maintenance work zones, including traffic control, the safe use of equipment, and the overall safety of workers, the traveling public, and the work environment.
5. **Scheduling work and equipment** -These questions test for knowledge of work scheduling principles and for the ability to arrange work and equipment assignments in a manner that will achieve work goals while staying within scheduling criteria. This may include setting up vacation or work schedules taking into consideration such factors as seniority, work skills, duty hours, and shift coverage.
6. **Understanding and interpreting plans, specifications, and technical instructions** - The questions test for the ability to comprehend, analyze, and perform computations based on technical drawings and written presentations related to construction and maintenance projects. All the information needed to answer the questions will be provided in the written material and/or drawings.

HOW TO TAKE A TEST

I. YOU MUST PASS AN EXAMINATION

A. WHAT EVERY CANDIDATE SHOULD KNOW

Examination applicants often ask us for help in preparing for the written test. What can I study in advance? What kinds of questions will be asked? How will the test be given? How will the papers be graded?

As an applicant for a civil service examination, you may be wondering about some of these things. Our purpose here is to suggest effective methods of advance study and to describe civil service examinations.

Your chances for success on this examination can be increased if you know how to prepare. Those "pre-examination jitters" can be reduced if you know what to expect. You can even experience an adventure in good citizenship if you know why civil service exams are given.

B. WHY ARE CIVIL SERVICE EXAMINATIONS GIVEN?

Civil service examinations are important to you in two ways. As a citizen, you want public jobs filled by employees who know how to do their work. As a job seeker, you want a fair chance to compete for that job on an equal footing with other candidates. The best-known means of accomplishing this two-fold goal is the competitive examination.

Exams are widely publicized throughout the nation. They may be administered for jobs in federal, state, city, municipal, town or village governments or agencies.

Any citizen may apply, with some limitations, such as the age or residence of applicants. Your experience and education may be reviewed to see whether you meet the requirements for the particular examination. When these requirements exist, they are reasonable and applied consistently to all applicants. Thus, a competitive examination may cause you some uneasiness now, but it is your privilege and safeguard.

C. HOW ARE CIVIL SERVICE EXAMS DEVELOPED?

Examinations are carefully written by trained technicians who are specialists in the field known as "psychological measurement," in consultation with recognized authorities in the field of work that the test will cover. These experts recommend the subject matter areas or skills to be tested; only those knowledges or skills important to your success on the job are included. The most reliable books and source materials available are used as references. Together, the experts and technicians judge the difficulty level of the questions.

Test technicians know how to phrase questions so that the problem is clearly stated. Their ethics do not permit "trick" or "catch" questions. Questions may have been tried out on sample groups, or subjected to statistical analysis, to determine their usefulness.

Written tests are often used in combination with performance tests, ratings of training and experience, and oral interviews. All of these measures combine to form the best-known means of finding the right person for the right job.

II. HOW TO PASS THE WRITTEN TEST

A. NATURE OF THE EXAMINATION

To prepare intelligently for civil service examinations, you should know how they differ from school examinations you have taken. In school you were assigned certain definite pages to read or subjects to cover. The examination questions were quite detailed and usually emphasized memory. Civil service exams, on the other hand, try to discover your present ability to perform the duties of a position, plus your potentiality to learn these duties. In other words, a civil service exam attempts to predict how successful you will be. Questions cover such a broad area that they cannot be as minute and detailed as school exam questions.

In the public service similar kinds of work, or positions, are grouped together in one "class." This process is known as *position-classification*. All the positions in a class are paid according to the salary range for that class. One class title covers all of these positions, and they are all tested by the same examination.

B. FOUR BASIC STEPS

1) Study the announcement

How, then, can you know what subjects to study? Our best answer is: "Learn as much as possible about the class of positions for which you've applied." The exam will test the knowledge, skills and abilities needed to do the work.

Your most valuable source of information about the position you want is the official exam announcement. This announcement lists the training and experience qualifications. Check these standards and apply only if you come reasonably close to meeting them.

The brief description of the position in the examination announcement offers some clues to the subjects which will be tested. Think about the job itself. Review the duties in your mind. Can you perform them, or are there some in which you are rusty? Fill in the blank spots in your preparation.

Many jurisdictions preview the written test in the exam announcement by including a section called "Knowledge and Abilities Required," "Scope of the Examination," or some similar heading. Here you will find out specifically what fields will be tested.

2) Review your own background

Once you learn in general what the position is all about, and what you need to know to do the work, ask yourself which subjects you already know fairly well and which need improvement. You may wonder whether to concentrate on improving your strong areas or on building some background in your fields of weakness. When the announcement has specified "some knowledge" or "considerable knowledge," or has used adjectives like "beginning principles of…" or "advanced … methods," you can get a clue as to the number and difficulty of questions to be asked in any given field. More questions, and hence broader coverage, would be included for those subjects which are more important in the work. Now weigh your strengths and weaknesses against the job requirements and prepare accordingly.

3) Determine the level of the position

Another way to tell how intensively you should prepare is to understand the level of the job for which you are applying. Is it the entering level? In other words, is this the position in which beginners in a field of work are hired? Or is it an intermediate or advanced level? Sometimes this is indicated by such words as "Junior" or "Senior" in the class title. Other jurisdictions use Roman numerals to designate the level – Clerk I, Clerk II, for example. The word "Supervisor" sometimes appears in the title. If the level is not indicated by the title, check the description of duties. Will you be working under very close supervision, or will you have responsibility for independent decisions in this work?

4) Choose appropriate study materials

Now that you know the subjects to be examined and the relative amount of each subject to be covered, you can choose suitable study materials. For beginning level jobs, or even advanced ones, if you have a pronounced weakness in some aspect of your training, read a modern, standard textbook in that field. Be sure it is up to date and has general coverage. Such books are normally available at your library, and the librarian will be glad to help you locate one. For entry-level positions, questions of appropriate difficulty are chosen -- neither highly advanced questions, nor those too simple. Such questions require careful thought but not advanced training.

If the position for which you are applying is technical or advanced, you will read more advanced, specialized material. If you are already familiar with the basic principles of your field, elementary textbooks would waste your time. Concentrate on advanced textbooks and technical periodicals. Think through the concepts and review difficult problems in your field.

These are all general sources. You can get more ideas on your own initiative, following these leads. For example, training manuals and publications of the government agency which employs workers in your field can be useful, particularly for technical and professional positions. A letter or visit to the government department involved may result in more specific study suggestions, and certainly will provide you with a more definite idea of the exact nature of the position you are seeking.

III. KINDS OF TESTS

Tests are used for purposes other than measuring knowledge and ability to perform specified duties. For some positions, it is equally important to test ability to make adjustments to new situations or to profit from training. In others, basic mental abilities not dependent on information are essential. Questions which test these things may not appear as pertinent to the duties of the position as those which test for knowledge and information. Yet they are often highly important parts of a fair examination. For very general questions, it is almost impossible to help you direct your study efforts. What we can do is to point out some of the more common of these general abilities needed in public service positions and describe some typical questions.

1) General information

Broad, general information has been found useful for predicting job success in some kinds of work. This is tested in a variety of ways, from vocabulary lists to questions about current events. Basic background in some field of work, such as sociology or economics, may be sampled in a group of questions. Often these are principles which have become familiar to most persons through exposure rather than through formal training. It is difficult to advise you how to study for these questions; being alert to the world around you is our best suggestion.

2) Verbal ability

An example of an ability needed in many positions is verbal or language ability. Verbal ability is, in brief, the ability to use and understand words. Vocabulary and grammar tests are typical measures of this ability. Reading comprehension or paragraph interpretation questions are common in many kinds of civil service tests. You are given a paragraph of written material and asked to find its central meaning.

3) Numerical ability

Number skills can be tested by the familiar arithmetic problem, by checking paired lists of numbers to see which are alike and which are different, or by interpreting charts and graphs. In the latter test, a graph may be printed in the test booklet which you are asked to use as the basis for answering questions.

4) Observation

A popular test for law-enforcement positions is the observation test. A picture is shown to you for several minutes, then taken away. Questions about the picture test your ability to observe both details and larger elements.

5) Following directions

In many positions in the public service, the employee must be able to carry out written instructions dependably and accurately. You may be given a chart with several columns, each column listing a variety of information. The questions require you to carry out directions involving the information given in the chart.

6) Skills and aptitudes

Performance tests effectively measure some manual skills and aptitudes. When the skill is one in which you are trained, such as typing or shorthand, you can practice. These tests are often very much like those given in business school or high school courses. For many of the other skills and aptitudes, however, no short-time preparation can be made. Skills and abilities natural to you or that you have developed throughout your lifetime are being tested.

Many of the general questions just described provide all the data needed to answer the questions and ask you to use your reasoning ability to find the answers. Your best preparation for these tests, as well as for tests of facts and ideas, is to be at your physical and mental best. You, no doubt, have your own methods of getting into an exam-taking mood and keeping "in shape." The next section lists some ideas on this subject.

IV. KINDS OF QUESTIONS

Only rarely is the "essay" question, which you answer in narrative form, used in civil service tests. Civil service tests are usually of the short-answer type. Full instructions for answering these questions will be given to you at the examination. But in case this is your first experience with short-answer questions and separate answer sheets, here is what you need to know:

1) Multiple-choice Questions

Most popular of the short-answer questions is the "multiple choice" or "best answer" question. It can be used, for example, to test for factual knowledge, ability to solve problems or judgment in meeting situations found at work.

A multiple-choice question is normally one of three types—
- It can begin with an incomplete statement followed by several possible endings. You are to find the one ending which *best* completes the statement, although some of the others may not be entirely wrong.
- It can also be a complete statement in the form of a question which is answered by choosing one of the statements listed.

- It can be in the form of a problem – again you select the best answer.

Here is an example of a multiple-choice question with a discussion which should give you some clues as to the method for choosing the right answer:

When an employee has a complaint about his assignment, the action which will *best* help him overcome his difficulty is to
- A. discuss his difficulty with his coworkers
- B. take the problem to the head of the organization
- C. take the problem to the person who gave him the assignment
- D. say nothing to anyone about his complaint

In answering this question, you should study each of the choices to find which is best. Consider choice "A" – Certainly an employee may discuss his complaint with fellow employees, but no change or improvement can result, and the complaint remains unresolved. Choice "B" is a poor choice since the head of the organization probably does not know what assignment you have been given, and taking your problem to him is known as "going over the head" of the supervisor. The supervisor, or person who made the assignment, is the person who can clarify it or correct any injustice. Choice "C" is, therefore, correct. To say nothing, as in choice "D," is unwise. Supervisors have and interest in knowing the problems employees are facing, and the employee is seeking a solution to his problem.

2) True/False Questions

The "true/false" or "right/wrong" form of question is sometimes used. Here a complete statement is given. Your job is to decide whether the statement is right or wrong.

SAMPLE: A roaming cell-phone call to a nearby city costs less than a non-roaming call to a distant city.

This statement is wrong, or false, since roaming calls are more expensive.

This is not a complete list of all possible question forms, although most of the others are variations of these common types. You will always get complete directions for answering questions. Be sure you understand *how* to mark your answers – ask questions until you do.

V. RECORDING YOUR ANSWERS

Computer terminals are used more and more today for many different kinds of exams.

For an examination with very few applicants, you may be told to record your answers in the test booklet itself. Separate answer sheets are much more common. If this separate answer sheet is to be scored by machine – and this is often the case – it is highly important that you mark your answers correctly in order to get credit.

An electronic scoring machine is often used in civil service offices because of the speed with which papers can be scored. Machine-scored answer sheets must be marked with a pencil, which will be given to you. This pencil has a high graphite content which responds to the electronic scoring machine. As a matter of fact, stray dots may register as answers, so do not let your pencil rest on the answer sheet while you are pondering the correct answer. Also, if your pencil lead breaks or is otherwise defective, ask for another.

Since the answer sheet will be dropped in a slot in the scoring machine, be careful not to bend the corners or get the paper crumpled.

The answer sheet normally has five vertical columns of numbers, with 30 numbers to a column. These numbers correspond to the question numbers in your test booklet. After each number, going across the page are four or five pairs of dotted lines. These short dotted lines have small letters or numbers above them. The first two pairs may also have a "T" or "F" above the letters. This indicates that the first two pairs only are to be used if the questions are of the true-false type. If the questions are multiple choice, disregard the "T" and "F" and pay attention only to the small letters or numbers.

Answer your questions in the manner of the sample that follows:

32. The largest city in the United States is
   A. Washington, D.C.
   B. New York City
   C. Chicago
   D. Detroit
   E. San Francisco

1) Choose the answer you think is best. (New York City is the largest, so "B" is correct.)
2) Find the row of dotted lines numbered the same as the question you are answering. (Find row number 32)
3) Find the pair of dotted lines corresponding to the answer. (Find the pair of lines under the mark "B.")
4) Make a solid black mark between the dotted lines.

VI. BEFORE THE TEST

Common sense will help you find procedures to follow to get ready for an examination. Too many of us, however, overlook these sensible measures. Indeed, nervousness and fatigue have been found to be the most serious reasons why applicants fail to do their best on civil service tests. Here is a list of reminders:

- Begin your preparation early – Don't wait until the last minute to go scurrying around for books and materials or to find out what the position is all about.
- Prepare continuously – An hour a night for a week is better than an all-night cram session. This has been definitely established. What is more, a night a week for a month will return better dividends than crowding your study into a shorter period of time.
- Locate the place of the exam – You have been sent a notice telling you when and where to report for the examination. If the location is in a different town or otherwise unfamiliar to you, it would be well to inquire the best route and learn something about the building.
- Relax the night before the test – Allow your mind to rest. Do not study at all that night. Plan some mild recreation or diversion; then go to bed early and get a good night's sleep.
- Get up early enough to make a leisurely trip to the place for the test – This way unforeseen events, traffic snarls, unfamiliar buildings, etc. will not upset you.
- Dress comfortably – A written test is not a fashion show. You will be known by number and not by name, so wear something comfortable.

- Leave excess paraphernalia at home – Shopping bags and odd bundles will get in your way. You need bring only the items mentioned in the official notice you received; usually everything you need is provided. Do not bring reference books to the exam. They will only confuse those last minutes and be taken away from you when in the test room.
- Arrive somewhat ahead of time – If because of transportation schedules you must get there very early, bring a newspaper or magazine to take your mind off yourself while waiting.
- Locate the examination room – When you have found the proper room, you will be directed to the seat or part of the room where you will sit. Sometimes you are given a sheet of instructions to read while you are waiting. Do not fill out any forms until you are told to do so; just read them and be prepared.
- Relax and prepare to listen to the instructions
- If you have any physical problem that may keep you from doing your best, be sure to tell the test administrator. If you are sick or in poor health, you really cannot do your best on the exam. You can come back and take the test some other time.

VII. AT THE TEST

The day of the test is here and you have the test booklet in your hand. The temptation to get going is very strong. Caution! There is more to success than knowing the right answers. You must know how to identify your papers and understand variations in the type of short-answer question used in this particular examination. Follow these suggestions for maximum results from your efforts:

1) Cooperate with the monitor
The test administrator has a duty to create a situation in which you can be as much at ease as possible. He will give instructions, tell you when to begin, check to see that you are marking your answer sheet correctly, and so on. He is not there to guard you, although he will see that your competitors do not take unfair advantage. He wants to help you do your best.

2) Listen to all instructions
Don't jump the gun! Wait until you understand all directions. In most civil service tests you get more time than you need to answer the questions. So don't be in a hurry. Read each word of instructions until you clearly understand the meaning. Study the examples, listen to all announcements and follow directions. Ask questions if you do not understand what to do.

3) Identify your papers
Civil service exams are usually identified by number only. You will be assigned a number; you must not put your name on your test papers. Be sure to copy your number correctly. Since more than one exam may be given, copy your exact examination title.

4) Plan your time
Unless you are told that a test is a "speed" or "rate of work" test, speed itself is usually not important. Time enough to answer all the questions will be provided, but this does not mean that you have all day. An overall time limit has been set. Divide the total time (in minutes) by the number of questions to determine the approximate time you have for each question.

5) Do not linger over difficult questions

If you come across a difficult question, mark it with a paper clip (useful to have along) and come back to it when you have been through the booklet. One caution if you do this – be sure to skip a number on your answer sheet as well. Check often to be sure that you have not lost your place and that you are marking in the row numbered the same as the question you are answering.

6) Read the questions

Be sure you know what the question asks! Many capable people are unsuccessful because they failed to *read* the questions correctly.

7) Answer all questions

Unless you have been instructed that a penalty will be deducted for incorrect answers, it is better to guess than to omit a question.

8) Speed tests

It is often better NOT to guess on speed tests. It has been found that on timed tests people are tempted to spend the last few seconds before time is called in marking answers at random – without even reading them – in the hope of picking up a few extra points. To discourage this practice, the instructions may warn you that your score will be "corrected" for guessing. That is, a penalty will be applied. The incorrect answers will be deducted from the correct ones, or some other penalty formula will be used.

9) Review your answers

If you finish before time is called, go back to the questions you guessed or omitted to give them further thought. Review other answers if you have time.

10) Return your test materials

If you are ready to leave before others have finished or time is called, take ALL your materials to the monitor and leave quietly. Never take any test material with you. The monitor can discover whose papers are not complete, and taking a test booklet may be grounds for disqualification.

VIII. EXAMINATION TECHNIQUES

1) Read the general instructions carefully. These are usually printed on the first page of the exam booklet. As a rule, these instructions refer to the timing of the examination; the fact that you should not start work until the signal and must stop work at a signal, etc. If there are any *special* instructions, such as a choice of questions to be answered, make sure that you note this instruction carefully.

2) When you are ready to start work on the examination, that is as soon as the signal has been given, read the instructions to each question booklet, underline any key words or phrases, such as *least, best, outline, describe* and the like. In this way you will tend to answer as requested rather than discover on reviewing your paper that you *listed without describing*, that you selected the *worst* choice rather than the *best* choice, etc.

3) If the examination is of the objective or multiple-choice type – that is, each question will also give a series of possible answers: A, B, C or D, and you are called upon to select the best answer and write the letter next to that answer on your answer paper – it is advisable to start answering each question in turn. There may be anywhere from 50 to 100 such questions in the three or four hours allotted and you can see how much time would be taken if you read through all the questions before beginning to answer any. Furthermore, if you come across a question or group of questions which you know would be difficult to answer, it would undoubtedly affect your handling of all the other questions.

4) If the examination is of the essay type and contains but a few questions, it is a moot point as to whether you should read all the questions before starting to answer any one. Of course, if you are given a choice – say five out of seven and the like – then it is essential to read all the questions so you can eliminate the two that are most difficult. If, however, you are asked to answer all the questions, there may be danger in trying to answer the easiest one first because you may find that you will spend too much time on it. The best technique is to answer the first question, then proceed to the second, etc.

5) Time your answers. Before the exam begins, write down the time it started, then add the time allowed for the examination and write down the time it must be completed, then divide the time available somewhat as follows:
    - If 3-1/2 hours are allowed, that would be 210 minutes. If you have 80 objective-type questions, that would be an average of 2-1/2 minutes per question. Allow yourself no more than 2 minutes per question, or a total of 160 minutes, which will permit about 50 minutes to review.
    - If for the time allotment of 210 minutes there are 7 essay questions to answer, that would average about 30 minutes a question. Give yourself only 25 minutes per question so that you have about 35 minutes to review.

6) The most important instruction is to *read each question* and make sure you know what is wanted. The second most important instruction is to *time yourself properly* so that you answer every question. The third most important instruction is to *answer every question*. Guess if you have to but include something for each question. Remember that you will receive no credit for a blank and will probably receive some credit if you write something in answer to an essay question. If you guess a letter – say "B" for a multiple-choice question – you may have guessed right. If you leave a blank as an answer to a multiple-choice question, the examiners may respect your feelings but it will not add a point to your score. Some exams may penalize you for wrong answers, so in such cases *only*, you may not want to guess unless you have some basis for your answer.

7) Suggestions
    a. Objective-type questions
        1. Examine the question booklet for proper sequence of pages and questions
        2. Read all instructions carefully
        3. Skip any question which seems too difficult; return to it after all other questions have been answered
        4. Apportion your time properly; do not spend too much time on any single question or group of questions

5. Note and underline key words – *all, most, fewest, least, best, worst, same, opposite*, etc.
6. Pay particular attention to negatives
7. Note unusual option, e.g., unduly long, short, complex, different or similar in content to the body of the question
8. Observe the use of "hedging" words – *probably, may, most likely*, etc.
9. Make sure that your answer is put next to the same number as the question
10. Do not second-guess unless you have good reason to believe the second answer is definitely more correct
11. Cross out original answer if you decide another answer is more accurate; do not erase until you are ready to hand your paper in
12. Answer all questions; guess unless instructed otherwise
13. Leave time for review

  b. Essay questions
    1. Read each question carefully
    2. Determine exactly what is wanted. Underline key words or phrases.
    3. Decide on outline or paragraph answer
    4. Include many different points and elements unless asked to develop any one or two points or elements
    5. Show impartiality by giving pros and cons unless directed to select one side only
    6. Make and write down any assumptions you find necessary to answer the questions
    7. Watch your English, grammar, punctuation and choice of words
    8. Time your answers; don't crowd material

8) Answering the essay question

Most essay questions can be answered by framing the specific response around several key words or ideas. Here are a few such key words or ideas:

M's: manpower, materials, methods, money, management
P's: purpose, program, policy, plan, procedure, practice, problems, pitfalls, personnel, public relations

  a. Six basic steps in handling problems:
    1. Preliminary plan and background development
    2. Collect information, data and facts
    3. Analyze and interpret information, data and facts
    4. Analyze and develop solutions as well as make recommendations
    5. Prepare report and sell recommendations
    6. Install recommendations and follow up effectiveness

  b. Pitfalls to avoid
    1. *Taking things for granted* – A statement of the situation does not necessarily imply that each of the elements is necessarily true; for example, a complaint may be invalid and biased so that all that can be taken for granted is that a complaint has been registered

2. *Considering only one side of a situation* – Wherever possible, indicate several alternatives and then point out the reasons you selected the best one
3. *Failing to indicate follow up* – Whenever your answer indicates action on your part, make certain that you will take proper follow-up action to see how successful your recommendations, procedures or actions turn out to be
4. *Taking too long in answering any single question* – Remember to time your answers properly

IX. AFTER THE TEST

Scoring procedures differ in detail among civil service jurisdictions although the general principles are the same. Whether the papers are hand-scored or graded by machine we have described, they are nearly always graded by number. That is, the person who marks the paper knows only the number – never the name – of the applicant. Not until all the papers have been graded will they be matched with names. If other tests, such as training and experience or oral interview ratings have been given, scores will be combined. Different parts of the examination usually have different weights. For example, the written test might count 60 percent of the final grade, and a rating of training and experience 40 percent. In many jurisdictions, veterans will have a certain number of points added to their grades.

After the final grade has been determined, the names are placed in grade order and an eligible list is established. There are various methods for resolving ties between those who get the same final grade – probably the most common is to place first the name of the person whose application was received first. Job offers are made from the eligible list in the order the names appear on it. You will be notified of your grade and your rank as soon as all these computations have been made. This will be done as rapidly as possible.

People who are found to meet the requirements in the announcement are called "eligibles." Their names are put on a list of eligible candidates. An eligible's chances of getting a job depend on how high he stands on this list and how fast agencies are filling jobs from the list.

When a job is to be filled from a list of eligibles, the agency asks for the names of people on the list of eligibles for that job. When the civil service commission receives this request, it sends to the agency the names of the three people highest on this list. Or, if the job to be filled has specialized requirements, the office sends the agency the names of the top three persons who meet these requirements from the general list.

The appointing officer makes a choice from among the three people whose names were sent to him. If the selected person accepts the appointment, the names of the others are put back on the list to be considered for future openings.

That is the rule in hiring from all kinds of eligible lists, whether they are for typist, carpenter, chemist, or something else. For every vacancy, the appointing officer has his choice of any one of the top three eligibles on the list. This explains why the person whose name is on top of the list sometimes does not get an appointment when some of the persons lower on the list do. If the appointing officer chooses the second or third eligible, the No. 1 eligible does not get a job at once, but stays on the list until he is appointed or the list is terminated.

X. HOW TO PASS THE INTERVIEW TEST

The examination for which you applied requires an oral interview test. You have already taken the written test and you are now being called for the interview test – the final part of the formal examination.

You may think that it is not possible to prepare for an interview test and that there are no procedures to follow during an interview. Our purpose is to point out some things you can do in advance that will help you and some good rules to follow and pitfalls to avoid while you are being interviewed.

What is an interview supposed to test?

The written examination is designed to test the technical knowledge and competence of the candidate; the oral is designed to evaluate intangible qualities, not readily measured otherwise, and to establish a list showing the relative fitness of each candidate – as measured against his competitors – for the position sought. Scoring is not on the basis of "right" and "wrong," but on a sliding scale of values ranging from "not passable" to "outstanding." As a matter of fact, it is possible to achieve a relatively low score without a single "incorrect" answer because of evident weakness in the qualities being measured.

Occasionally, an examination may consist entirely of an oral test – either an individual or a group oral. In such cases, information is sought concerning the technical knowledges and abilities of the candidate, since there has been no written examination for this purpose. More commonly, however, an oral test is used to supplement a written examination.

Who conducts interviews?

The composition of oral boards varies among different jurisdictions. In nearly all, a representative of the personnel department serves as chairman. One of the members of the board may be a representative of the department in which the candidate would work. In some cases, "outside experts" are used, and, frequently, a businessman or some other representative of the general public is asked to serve. Labor and management or other special groups may be represented. The aim is to secure the services of experts in the appropriate field.

However the board is composed, it is a good idea (and not at all improper or unethical) to ascertain in advance of the interview who the members are and what groups they represent. When you are introduced to them, you will have some idea of their backgrounds and interests, and at least you will not stutter and stammer over their names.

What should be done before the interview?

While knowledge about the board members is useful and takes some of the surprise element out of the interview, there is other preparation which is more substantive. It *is* possible to prepare for an oral interview – in several ways:

1) Keep a copy of your application and review it carefully before the interview

This may be the only document before the oral board, and the starting point of the interview. Know what education and experience you have listed there, and the sequence and dates of all of it. Sometimes the board will ask you to review the highlights of your experience for them; you should not have to hem and haw doing it.

2) Study the class specification and the examination announcement

Usually, the oral board has one or both of these to guide them. The qualities, characteristics or knowledges required by the position sought are stated in these documents. They offer valuable clues as to the nature of the oral interview. For example, if the job involves supervisory responsibilities, the announcement will usually indicate that knowledge of modern supervisory methods and the qualifications of the candidate as a supervisor will be tested. If so, you can expect such questions, frequently in the form of a hypothetical situation which you are expected to solve. NEVER go into an oral without knowledge of the duties and responsibilities of the job you seek.

3) Think through each qualification required

Try to visualize the kind of questions you would ask if you were a board member. How well could you answer them? Try especially to appraise your own knowledge and background in each area, *measured against the job sought*, and identify any areas in which you are weak. Be critical and realistic – do not flatter yourself.

4) Do some general reading in areas in which you feel you may be weak

For example, if the job involves supervision and your past experience has NOT, some general reading in supervisory methods and practices, particularly in the field of human relations, might be useful. Do NOT study agency procedures or detailed manuals. The oral board will be testing your understanding and capacity, not your memory.

5) Get a good night's sleep and watch your general health and mental attitude

You will want a clear head at the interview. Take care of a cold or any other minor ailment, and of course, no hangovers.

What should be done on the day of the interview?

Now comes the day of the interview itself. Give yourself plenty of time to get there. Plan to arrive somewhat ahead of the scheduled time, particularly if your appointment is in the fore part of the day. If a previous candidate fails to appear, the board might be ready for you a bit early. By early afternoon an oral board is almost invariably behind schedule if there are many candidates, and you may have to wait. Take along a book or magazine to read, or your application to review, but leave any extraneous material in the waiting room when you go in for your interview. In any event, relax and compose yourself.

The matter of dress is important. The board is forming impressions about you – from your experience, your manners, your attitude, and your appearance. Give your personal appearance careful attention. Dress your best, but not your flashiest. Choose conservative, appropriate clothing, and be sure it is immaculate. This is a business interview, and your appearance should indicate that you regard it as such. Besides, being well groomed and properly dressed will help boost your confidence.

Sooner or later, someone will call your name and escort you into the interview room. *This is it.* From here on you are on your own. It is too late for any more preparation. But remember, you asked for this opportunity to prove your fitness, and you are here because your request was granted.

What happens when you go in?

The usual sequence of events will be as follows: The clerk (who is often the board stenographer) will introduce you to the chairman of the oral board, who will introduce you to the other members of the board. Acknowledge the introductions before you sit down. Do not be surprised if you find a microphone facing you or a stenotypist sitting by. Oral interviews are usually recorded in the event of an appeal or other review.

Usually the chairman of the board will open the interview by reviewing the highlights of your education and work experience from your application – primarily for the benefit of the other members of the board, as well as to get the material into the record. Do not interrupt or comment unless there is an error or significant misinterpretation; if that is the case, do not hesitate. But do not quibble about insignificant matters. Also, he will usually ask you some question about your education, experience or your present job – partly to get you to start talking and to establish the interviewing "rapport." He may start the actual questioning, or turn it over to one of the other members. Frequently, each member undertakes the questioning on a particular area, one in which he is perhaps most competent, so you can expect each member to participate in the examination. Because time is limited, you may also expect some rather abrupt switches in the direction the questioning takes, so do not be upset by it. Normally, a board member will not pursue a single line of questioning unless he discovers a particular strength or weakness.

After each member has participated, the chairman will usually ask whether any member has any further questions, then will ask you if you have anything you wish to add. Unless you are expecting this question, it may floor you. Worse, it may start you off on an extended, extemporaneous speech. The board is not usually seeking more information. The question is principally to offer you a last opportunity to present further qualifications or to indicate that you have nothing to add. So, if you feel that a significant qualification or characteristic has been overlooked, it is proper to point it out in a sentence or so. Do not compliment the board on the thoroughness of their examination – they have been sketchy, and you know it. If you wish, merely say, "No thank you, I have nothing further to add." This is a point where you can "talk yourself out" of a good impression or fail to present an important bit of information. Remember, *you close the interview yourself.*

The chairman will then say, "That is all, Mr. _____, thank you." Do not be startled; the interview is over, and quicker than you think. Thank him, gather your belongings and take your leave. Save your sigh of relief for the other side of the door.

How to put your best foot forward
Throughout this entire process, you may feel that the board individually and collectively is trying to pierce your defenses, seek out your hidden weaknesses and embarrass and confuse you. Actually, this is not true. They are obliged to make an appraisal of your qualifications for the job you are seeking, and they want to see you in your best light. Remember, they must interview all candidates and a non-cooperative candidate may become a failure in spite of their best efforts to bring out his qualifications. Here are 15 suggestions that will help you:

1) **Be natural – Keep your attitude confident, not cocky**
If you are not confident that you can do the job, do not expect the board to be. Do not apologize for your weaknesses, try to bring out your strong points. The board is interested in a positive, not negative, presentation. Cockiness will antagonize any board member and make him wonder if you are covering up a weakness by a false show of strength.

2) **Get comfortable, but don't lounge or sprawl**
Sit erectly but not stiffly. A careless posture may lead the board to conclude that you are careless in other things, or at least that you are not impressed by the importance of the occasion. Either conclusion is natural, even if incorrect. Do not fuss with your clothing, a pencil or an ashtray. Your hands may occasionally be useful to emphasize a point; do not let them become a point of distraction.

3) **Do not wisecrack or make small talk**
This is a serious situation, and your attitude should show that you consider it as such. Further, the time of the board is limited – they do not want to waste it, and neither should you.

4) Do not exaggerate your experience or abilities

In the first place, from information in the application or other interviews and sources, the board may know more about you than you think. Secondly, you probably will not get away with it. An experienced board is rather adept at spotting such a situation, so do not take the chance.

5) If you know a board member, do not make a point of it, yet do not hide it

Certainly you are not fooling him, and probably not the other members of the board. Do not try to take advantage of your acquaintanceship – it will probably do you little good.

6) Do not dominate the interview

Let the board do that. They will give you the clues – do not assume that you have to do all the talking. Realize that the board has a number of questions to ask you, and do not try to take up all the interview time by showing off your extensive knowledge of the answer to the first one.

7) Be attentive

You only have 20 minutes or so, and you should keep your attention at its sharpest throughout. When a member is addressing a problem or question to you, give him your undivided attention. Address your reply principally to him, but do not exclude the other board members.

8) Do not interrupt

A board member may be stating a problem for you to analyze. He will ask you a question when the time comes. Let him state the problem, and wait for the question.

9) Make sure you understand the question

Do not try to answer until you are sure what the question is. If it is not clear, restate it in your own words or ask the board member to clarify it for you. However, do not haggle about minor elements.

10) Reply promptly but not hastily

A common entry on oral board rating sheets is "candidate responded readily," or "candidate hesitated in replies." Respond as promptly and quickly as you can, but do not jump to a hasty, ill-considered answer.

11) Do not be peremptory in your answers

A brief answer is proper – but do not fire your answer back. That is a losing game from your point of view. The board member can probably ask questions much faster than you can answer them.

12) Do not try to create the answer you think the board member wants

He is interested in what kind of mind you have and how it works – not in playing games. Furthermore, he can usually spot this practice and will actually grade you down on it.

13) Do not switch sides in your reply merely to agree with a board member

Frequently, a member will take a contrary position merely to draw you out and to see if you are willing and able to defend your point of view. Do not start a debate, yet do not surrender a good position. If a position is worth taking, it is worth defending.

14) Do not be afraid to admit an error in judgment if you are shown to be wrong

The board knows that you are forced to reply without any opportunity for careful consideration. Your answer may be demonstrably wrong. If so, admit it and get on with the interview.

15) Do not dwell at length on your present job

The opening question may relate to your present assignment. Answer the question but do not go into an extended discussion. You are being examined for a *new* job, not your present one. As a matter of fact, try to phrase ALL your answers in terms of the job for which you are being examined.

Basis of Rating

Probably you will forget most of these "do's" and "don'ts" when you walk into the oral interview room. Even remembering them all will not ensure you a passing grade. Perhaps you did not have the qualifications in the first place. But remembering them will help you to put your best foot forward, without treading on the toes of the board members.

Rumor and popular opinion to the contrary notwithstanding, an oral board wants you to make the best appearance possible. They know you are under pressure – but they also want to see how you respond to it as a guide to what your reaction would be under the pressures of the job you seek. They will be influenced by the degree of poise you display, the personal traits you show and the manner in which you respond.

ABOUT THIS BOOK

This book contains tests divided into Examination Sections. Go through each test, answering every question in the margin. We have also attached a sample answer sheet at the back of the book that can be removed and used. At the end of each test look at the answer key and check your answers. On the ones you got wrong, look at the right answer choice and learn. Do not fill in the answers first. Do not memorize the questions and answers, but understand the answer and principles involved. On your test, the questions will likely be different from the samples. Questions are changed and new ones added. If you understand these past questions you should have success with any changes that arise. Tests may consist of several types of questions. We have additional books on each subject should more study be advisable or necessary for you. Finally, the more you study, the better prepared you will be. This book is intended to be the last thing you study before you walk into the examination room. Prior study of relevant texts is also recommended. NLC publishes some of these in our Fundamental Series. Knowledge and good sense are important factors in passing your exam. Good luck also helps. So now study this Passbook, absorb the material contained within and take that knowledge into the examination. Then do your best to pass that exam.

EXAMINATION SECTION

EXAMINATION SECTION
TEST 1

DIRECTIONS: Each question or incomplete statement is followed by several suggested answers or completions. Select the one that BEST answers the question or completes the statement. *PRINT THE LETTER OF THE CORRECT ANSWER IN THE SPACE AT THE RIGHT.*

1. On the monthly report of the amount of work completed, the units used to measure the amount of work completed on guardrails and beam barriers installed on arterial highways is

    A. square feet
    B. square yards
    C. linear feet
    D. linear yards

2. On the daily work report for the sidewalk concrete gang is a formula, $M = [G - (D + U)]$, where G = total man-hours worked, D = total man-hours delays, U = total man-hours unmeasured work, and M = total man-hours measured work.
If G = 98, D = 42, U = 21, then M is equal to

    A. 35   B. 56   C. 77   D. 119

3. When a plumber *opens a street*, he is responsible for restoring the pavement. After completion of the permanent restoration, the plumber is responsible for maintaining the restored area for a total period of

    A. six months
    B. one year
    C. one year and 6 months
    D. two years

4. A permit for a street opening may be issued for a single permit activity for one block length up to a MAXIMUM length of _____ feet.

    A. 50   B. 100   C. 200   D. 300

5. A street obstruction bond taken out by a contractor working in the street is to insure the city if

    A. a pedestrian is injured by material stored on the sidewalk
    B. an automobile is damaged by material stored in the street
    C. curbs, sidewalks, and pavements are damaged
    D. obstructions, illegally placed in the street, must be removed

6. On the daily work report for the sidewalk concrete gang is an item *curb*.
The different types of curb listed on the report are: bluestone or granite, concrete-steel face, concrete-regular face, and

    A. drop
    B. paving block
    C. concrete block
    D. prefabricated

7. On the monthly report of work output under time (manhours) is a column headed MSO, which refers to manhours

    A. of mechanical services operator other than MVO
    B. of operation time lost while waiting
    C. of operation time lost due to the weather
    D. spent operating mechanical equipment by the MVO

8. In the city, concrete sidewalks are required to have a minimum thickness of concrete of _____ inches.

   A. 3 B. 4 C. 5 D. 6

9. Asphalt was laid for a length of 210 feet on the entire width of a street whose curb-to-curb distance is 30 feet. The number of square yards covered with asphalt is MOST NEARLY

   A. 210 B. 700 C. 2100 D. 6300

10. A layer of cinders is used as a base for a concrete sidewalk.
    The MAIN purpose of the cinders is to

    A. act as an air entraining agent for the concrete in the sidewalk
    B. replace poor soil under the sidewalk
    C. provide drainage under the sidewalk
    D. cushion the sidewalk when heavy loads are placed on the sidewalk

11. The unit used on the daily gang report to report the amount of measurement of debris removed is

    A. square foot B. square yard
    C. cubic foot D. cubic yard

12. 627 cubic feet contains MOST NEARLY _____ cubic yards.

    A. 21 B. 22 C. 23 D. 24

13. Of the following, the one that is INCORRECT curb construction is a curb made

    A. with a height of 5 inches
    B. with a steel angle for the face
    C. without a steel face
    D. monolithically with the sidewalk

14. Where feasible, concrete sidewalk panels should be made in squares of _____ feet by _____ feet.

    A. 3; 3 B. 5; 5 C. 6; 6 D. 7; 7

15. The steel facing for concrete curbs are splayed

    A. at an expansion joint
    B. where it butts against an adjacent steel plate
    C. at a drop curb
    D. at a radius bend

16. Expansion joints in steel curb facing shall be 1/4 inch wide and shall be filled with

    A. sand B. premolded filler
    C. poured asphalt D. dry pack

17. One inch is MOST NEARLY equal to _____ feet.

    A. 0.8 B. 0.08 C. 0.008 D. 0.0008

18. Of the following, the *final* finish on a sidewalk is MOST frequently made with a

    A. wood float
    B. screed
    C. steel trowel
    D. darby

19. An air entraining compound would be added to concrete MAINLY to

    A. make the concrete lighter
    B. make the concrete cure faster
    C. improve the resistance of the concrete to frost action
    D. increase the tensile strength of the concrete

20. *ASTM,* as used in specifications for concrete, is an abbreviation for the

    A. American Society for Testing Materials
    B. American Standard Training Manual
    C. American Standard Testing Materials
    D. Association of Scientists for Testing Materials

21. A 15-foot-wide sidewalk has a pitch of 1/4 inch per foot. The difference in elevation from the curb to 15 feet from the curb in the direction of the pitch is _____ inches.

    A. 3 B. 3 3/4 C. 4 D. 4 1/2

22. A liquid asphalt is designated *RC70.*
    The letters RC stand for

    A. Rough Course
    B. Rubber Cement
    C. Rapid Curing
    D. Reinforced Concrete

23. Unless otherwise specified, steel faced concrete curb shall consist of the steel curb facing in _____ -foot lengths.

    A. 5 B. 10 C. 15 D. 20

24. The difference between sheet asphalt and asphaltic concrete is that sheet asphalt

    A. contains no sand while asphaltic concrete contains sand
    B. contains no coarse aggregate while asphaltic concrete contains coarse aggregate
    C. contains no mineral filler while asphaltic concrete contains mineral filler
    D. has no flux while asphaltic concrete has flux

25. An approved roller shall weigh not less than 225 pounds per inch width of main roll. If the main roll width is 60 inches, the MINIMUM roller weight shall be equal to or greater than _____ lbs.

    A. 12,000 B. 12,500 C. 13,000 D. 13,500

KEY (CORRECT ANSWERS)

1. C
2. A
3. D
4. D
5. C

6. A
7. A
8. B
9. B
10. C

11. D
12. C
13. D
14. B
15. C

16. B
17. B
18. A
19. C
20. A

21. B
22. C
23. D
24. B
25. D

TEST 2

DIRECTIONS: Each question or incomplete statement is followed by several suggested answers or completions. Select the one that BEST answers the question or completes the statement. *PRINT THE LETTER OF THE CORRECT ANSWER IN THE SPACE AT THE RIGHT.*

1. A specification states that the rate of application of asphalt cement shall be 1 1/2 gallons per square yard with a tolerance of 1/10 of a gallon.
   Of the following, the rate of application that would be acceptable is _____ gallons per square yard.

   A. 1.2   B. 1.3   C. 1.6   D. 1.7

2. Of the following, the BEST reason for compacting backfill is to

   A. prevent settlement   B. crush oversized rocks
   C. facilitate drainage   D. make the soil uniform

3. Asphalt block is hexagonal tile block.
   The number of vertical sides of each block in place is

   A. 4   B. 6   C. 8   D. 10

4. Concrete driveways shall have a MINIMUM thickness of concrete of _____ inches.

   A. 5   B. 6   C. 7   D. 8

5. When the tops of manholes must be raised because of repaving, the MOST practical of the following methods to use is to

   A. break out the manhole frame and replace it with a deeper frame
   B. remove the manhole frame, build up the top of the manhole with bricks, and reset the frame
   C. use a thicker manhole cover
   D. place a metal collar on top of the existing frame

6. In a 1:2:4 concrete mix, the 2 indicates the quantity of

   A. water   B. sand   C. cement   D. aggregate

7. A tree pit shall be located in the area immediately in back of the curb.
   The MAXIMUM size of the tree pit shall be

   A. 3' x 3'   B. 4' x 4'   C. 5' x 5'   D. 6' x 6'

8. A temporary asphaltic pavement is placed over an excavation in the street by a private contractor.
   The MINIMUM required thickness of the finish course of the temporary asphaltic pavement is _____ inch(es).

   A. 1   B. 2   C. 3   D. 4

9. When a vault is abandoned, it must be filled in with clean incombustible materials, well-tamped.
   Where such structures adjoin the curb of a street, the roof must be removed and the enclosing walls cut down below the curb to a depth of _____ feet.

   A. 2   B. 4   C. 6   D. 8

10. Granite curbs are required to be set on a cradle. The MAIN purpose of the cradle is to

   A. prevent cracking of the curb
   B. prevent settling of the curb
   C. help keep the curb in line while it is being set
   D. separate the curb from the adjacent sidewalk

11. Paving was installed on a street from Station 3+15 to Station 4+90.
    The length of street that was paved is _____ feet.

   A. 75   B. 115   C. 175   D. 215

12. A district foreman uses an engineer's tape and measures a distance of 26.50 feet.
    This distance is equal to _____ feet _____ inch(es).

   A. 26; 5   B. 26; 6   C. 26; 1/2   D. 26; 0.6

13. Written on a can containing material delivered from a manufacturer is the notation
    Approved by the B.S. & A.
    The B.S. & A. is an abbreviation for the

   A. Bureau of Shipping and Allocation
   B. Board of Standards and Appeals
   C. Board of Supervision and Approval
   D. Bureau of Supervision and Assistance

14. An asphalt macadam pavement consists of a base course and a wearing course.
    The purpose of the base course is to

   A. provide drainage
   B. provide a level surface for the wearing course
   C. spread the load from the surface when it reaches the soil
   D. replace defective soil

15. Of the following, the MOST important recent advancement in power-driven equipment and tools is

   A. reduction in weight of the equipment
   B. improved surface finish
   C. higher operating speed
   D. lower noise levels

16. A wooden horse, used to warn traffic away, should be placed in front of which of the following defects in the street?
    A

   A. broken curb
   B. piece of roadway pavement that is very thin and the pavement whose base is starting to show through
   C. very badly broken manhole cover in the center of the street
   D. catch basin filled to the surface with debris

17. When a street is to be paved, the roller should

    A. start at the curb, go the length of the street and then move toward the center
    B. move from curb to curb transversely across the street
    C. start at the center, go the length of the street, and then move toward the curb
    D. roll at all the manhole covers first and then start rolling the length of the street

18. The use of long chutes to place concrete for a road base is usually prohibited.
    The BEST of the following reasons for prohibiting long chutes in this case is that

    A. the concrete will set by the time it is in place
    B. the water will evaporate from the mix
    C. segregation of the aggregate will occur
    D. the stone will be broken down into smaller particles

19. When sheet asphalt is spread by hand, the speed of the rolling should NOT exceed _____ square yards per hour.

    A. 100   B. 300   C. 500   D. 700

20. Of the following, the BEST way to insure long trouble-free operation of mechanical equipment is by periodic inspection and

    A. use
    B. servicing
    C. painting
    D. rotation of operators

21. Of the following maintenance work, the one type that is LEAST likely to be done by your agency on mechanical equipment is

    A. tune-up
    B. repairing
    C. overhauling
    D. rebuilding

22. Of the following, the MOST important equipment needed to lay sheet asphalt pavement is truck, roller, fire wagon, and

    A. grader
    B. distributor
    C. planer
    D. spreader

23. Of the following, the BEST reason why deep potholes should be repaired *immediately* is that

    A. they look bad
    B. they are a safety hazard
    C. they present a drainage problem
    D. people complaining about unfilled potholes cause unfavorable publicity

24. Of the following, the MOST serious safety hazard on highway and street maintenance work is

    A. injury from flying debris during pavement breaking
    B. motor traffic
    C. working close to trucks, bulldozers, and rollers
    D. cave-ins

25. Of the following, the BEST way a laborer can avoid accidents is to

   A. work slowly
   B. be alert
   C. wear safety shoes
   D. wear glasses

26. Of the following, the BEST first aid treatment for a second degree burn is to cover the burn with a _____ sterile dressing.

   A. thin, wet
   B. thin, dry
   C. thick, wet
   D. thick, dry

27. One of the laborers on the job feels unusually tired, has a headache and nausea, is perspiring heavily, and the skin is pale and clammy.
   He is probably suffering from

   A. epilepsy
   B. food poisoning
   C. heat exhaustion
   D. sunstroke

28. If a laborer feels faint, the BEST advice to give him is to advise him to

   A. lie flat with his head low
   B. walk around till he revives
   C. run around till he revives
   D. drink a glass of cold water

29. Of the following types of fire extinguisher, the one to use on an electrical fire is

   A. soda acid
   B. carbon dioxide
   C. water pump tank
   D. pyrene

30. The GREATEST number of injuries from equipment used in construction work result from

   A. carelessness of the operator
   B. poor maintenance of the equipment
   C. overloading of the equipment
   D. poor inspection of the equipment

KEY (CORRECT ANSWERS)

1.	C	16.	C
2.	A	17.	A
3.	B	18.	C
4.	C	19.	B
5.	D	20.	B
6.	B	21.	D
7.	C	22.	D
8.	C	23.	B
9.	A	24.	B
10.	B	25.	B
11.	C	26.	D
12.	B	27.	C
13.	B	28.	A
14.	C	29.	B
15.	D	30.	A

EXAMINATION SECTION
TEST 1

DIRECTIONS: Each question or incomplete statement is followed by several suggested answers or completions. Select the one that BEST answers the question or completes the statement. *PRINT THE LETTER OF THE CORRECT ANSWER IN THE SPACE AT THE RIGHT.*

1. Asphalt is derived mainly

    A. as a byproduct from the production of coke
    B. from asphalt deposits seeping to the surface of the earth
    C. from the refining of crude oil
    D. from bituminous coal

2. Cutback liquid asphalts are prepared by blending asphalt with a volatile solvent. The one of the following that is NOT used as an asphalt solvent is

    A. naphtha   B. gasoline   C. kerosene   D. toluene

3. The primary purpose of the solvent in cutback asphalt is to allow the

    A. use of a larger size aggregate in the mix
    B. application of the asphalt at a relatively low temperature
    C. application of asphalt in wet weather
    D. application of asphalt in hot weather

4. The thickness of the sheet asphalt on a sheet asphalt pavement is usually _____ inch(es).

    A. 1/2 inch to 3/4   B. 1 inch to 1 1/2
    C. 1 5/8 inches to 2   D. 2 1/4 inches to 3

5. The grade of an asphalt cement is designated as AR4000.
   The AR is an abbreviation for

    A. asphalt rating   B. acid resistance
    C. aged residue   D. aging resistance

6. An asphaltic emulsion is a suspension of asphalt in

    A. kerosene   B. gasoline   C. toluene   D. water

7. A very light application of asphalt on an existing paved surface will promote bond between this surface and the subsequent course is known as a(n) _____ coat.

    A. prime   B. adhesion
    C. tack   D. penetrating

8. Of the following, payment is usually made for asphalt pavements at the contract price per

    A. square inch   B. square foot
    C. square yard   D. 100 square feet

9. The grade of an asphalt cement is designated AR4000. The 4000 is a measure of

   A. strength B. viscosity C. ductility D. density

10. Of the following, the geometric shape of a horizontal curve on a highway is

    A. parabolic
    B. hyperbolic
    C. circular
    D. elliptical

11. A borrow pit in highway construction is used

    A. for storing stormwater in a heavy rain
    B. for coarse aggregate in Portland cement concrete
    C. for coarse aggregate in asphalt concrete
    D. to obtain fill for embankments

12. Overhaul in highway construction is usually measured and paid for by the

    A. yard - cubic foot
    B. yard - cubic yard
    C. station - cubic foot
    D. station - cubic yard

13. A Benkelman beam is used in highway work

    A. as an indicator of the ability of a pavement to withstand loading
    B. to measure the roughness of an asphalt concrete pavement
    C. to measure the uniformity of an asphalt concrete pavement
    D. to measure the ability of an asphalt concrete pavement to remain serviceable if the subgrade is undermined

14. When surfacing over an existing pavement, of the following, the MOST practical way to insure that the required thickness of new pavement is met is

    A. expansion of clay when exposed to water
    B. expansion of soil when excavated
    C. waviness in a soil embankment when being compacted with a roller
    D. expansion of loamy soil when exposed to water

15. When surfacing over an existing pavement, of the following, the MOST practical way to insure that the required thickness of new pavement is met is

    A. have wood blocks of the thickness of the new pavement temporarily placed on the existing pavement to insure that the thickness requirements will be met at the time of paving
    B. make a survey of the existing pavement elevations and a survey of the final pavement elevations and check that the thickness requirements are met
    C. check that the amount of asphalt delivered is adequate to meet the depth requirements of the area to be paved
    D. take core borings to determine if the thickness meets specifications

16. The maximum roller speed for steel tired rollers paving asphalt concrete is a maximum of _____ mile(s) per hour.

    A. 7 B. 5 C. 3 D. 1

17. The weathered or dry surface appearing on a relatively new pavement can generally be attributed to

    A. inadequate rolling
    B. oversized coarse aggregate in the mix
    C. excessive amount of fine aggregate
    D. insufficient asphalt in the mix

18. Construction contracts for highways have items paid either by unit price or lump sum. The one of the following that is usually a lump sum item on a highway contract is

    A. excavation   B. paving
    C. fencing   D. demolition

19. Highway roadway subgrades are usually required to have a relative density of _____ percent.

    A. 80 to 84   B. 85 to 89   C. 90 to 95   D. 100

20. A *profile* of a highway is

    A. the section taken along the centerline of the highway
    B. an aesthetic landscape sketch of the highway
    C. used to determine the line of the highway
    D. used to locate overpasses

21. A culvert as used under a highway is usually installed

    A. as a relief sewer
    B. as a bypass for a stream
    C. in a stream bed
    D. to carry sanitary and storm flow

22. A mass diagram as related to highway construction work is used to

    A. minimize traffic congestion
    B. compute payment for hauling excavation and fill
    C. find the largest feasible radius of curvature for a horizontal curve
    D. help determine the depth of an asphalt concrete pavement

23. The geometric shape of a vertical curve on a highway is a(n)

    A. parabola   B. hyperbola   C. circle   D. ellipse

24. When cast iron bell and spigot pipe is used in sewer construction, the joint is usually sealed with

    A. lead   B. tin
    C. cement mortar   D. oakum

25. A planimeter is used to measure

    A. location   B. area   C. elevation   D. angles

KEY (CORRECT ANSWERS)

1. C
2. D
3. B
4. B
5. C

6. D
7. C
8. B
9. B
10. C

11. D
12. D
13. A
14. B
15. A

16. C
17. D
18. D
19. C
20. A

21. C
22. B
23. A
24. A
25. B

TEST 2

DIRECTIONS: Each question or incomplete statement is followed by several suggested answers or completions. Select the one that BEST answers the question or completes the statement. *PRINT THE LETTER OF THE CORRECT ANSWER IN THE SPACE AT THE RIGHT.*

1. A witness stake is usually used in surveying primarily as

    A. proof that a given location has been surveyed
    B. an aid in locating a surveying stake
    C. a marker to prevent a stake being disturbed
    D. an offset stake

2. Before the contractor begins work on a sewer or highway project, a detailed survey is made of all existing structures that may be affected by the construction in order to

    A. protect against false claims for damage
    B. insure that the contractor causes no damage to property
    C. insure that existing elevations conform to elevations on the contract drawings
    D. uncover potential weaknesses in structures

3. The optimum moisture content of a given soil will result in the

    A. plastic limit of the soil is reached
    B. liquid limit of the soil is reached
    C. porosity of the soil is at its maximum
    D. soil is compacted to its maximum dry density

4. The letters SC for soil means

    A. silty clay   B. clayey sand
    C. sandy clay   D. clayey silt

5. A cradle is used under a large precast circular concrete pipe sewer. The purpose of the cradle is mainly to

    A. minimize the settlement of the earth on the sides of the sewer
    B. minimize the settlement under the pipe
    C. strengthen the pipe against collapse
    D. resist side pressure against the pipe

6. The joints on laid precast concrete pipe were poorly made. The consequence of this poor workmanship is most likely

    A. the pipe will settle
    B. the pipe may collapse
    C. the water table may be adversely affected
    D. there will be excessive infiltration

7. An existing sewer is to connect into a new deep manhole for a new sewer. According to old plans for the existing sewer, the elevation of the existing sewer is 1/2 inch lower than shown on the plan.
Of the following, the BEST action that the inspector can take is

A. call his superior for instructions
B. do nothing
C. have the contractor relay the existing pipe to the theoretical elevation shown on the old plan
D. have an adjustable connection placed between the old pipe and the new manhole

8. The contractor proposes using a cement-lime mix for cement mortar to be used in building a manhole.
This is

A. *good* practice as this is a more workable mortar
B. *good* practice as the mortar is slow setting
C. *poor* practice because the mortar weakens in a wet environment
D. *poor* practice as a cement-lime mortar is more porous than a cement mortar

9. Most serious claims for extra payment on large sewer contracts result from

A. soil conditions that are markedly different from those that were presented by the owner
B. the inspectors being unreasonable in their demands
C. delay in making the areas available for work
D. the fact that the method of construction required by the owner proved to be unworkable

10. Unconsolidated fill is at pipe laying depth. Of the following, the BEST action that an inspector can take is to

A. have the unconsolidated fill removed and replaced with concrete
B. have the unconsolidated fill removed and replaced with sound fill
C. report this matter to your supervisor for his consideration
D. ask the contractor to consolidate the fill

11. Buried debris not shown on the borings is uncovered near the surface of an excavation for a deep sewer. Of the following, the BEST action for an inspector to take is to

A. record the depth and extent of the debris in the event of a claim
B. do nothing as this has no effect on the final product
C. notify the contractor that there is no valid claim for the extra work required
D. be certain that the debris is not used in the backfill

12. A come-along or deadman is sometimes used in the laying of large precast concrete pipe to insure

A. the pipe is at proper grade
B. the pipe is on proper line
C. that the pipe will not subsequently settle
D. that the pipe is properly seated

13. In laying sewers,

A. accuracy in the line of the sewer is more important than accuracy in the grade of the sewer
B. accuracy in the grade of the sewer is more important than accuracy in the line of the sewer

C. accuracy in the line and grade of the sewer are equally important
D. since the sewer is underground, accuracy is not required either for line or grade

14. A sewer contract is given out with a price per foot of sewer for different diameter sewers. After the contract is let, the low bidder is required to give a breakdown of his price per foot of sewer to include excavation, sewer in place, backfill, and restoration. The purpose of this breakdown is to

    A. facilitate partial payments
    B. insure the bid is not unbalanced
    C. enable the agency to gather up-to-date cost data for future projects
    D. make it easier to price extra work

14.____

15. The house sewer runs from the house to the main line sewer. The size of this sewer is most frequently _____ inches.

    A. 4   B. 5   C. 6   D. 8

15.____

16. A line on centerline at the inside bottom of a pipe or conduit is known as the

    A. convert   B. invert   C. subvert   D. exvert

16.____

17. One of the most important elements of excavating for sewer construction is to maintain the specified width of the trench at the top of the pipe. If the width at the top of the pipe is too great,

    A. this may cause excessive settlement of the pipe
    B. this may cause excessive settlement of the backfill damaging the final pavement
    C. this may place excessive load on the pipe
    D. it may undermine utilities adjacent to the pipe

17.____

18. Wellpoints are used in sewer construction mainly to

    A. keep water out of the trench due to a heavy rainstorm
    B. keep water out of the excavation and subsoil to avoid excessive pressure on the sheeting
    C. prevent a boil from forming in the trench
    D. lower the water table to facilitate construction of the sewer

18.____

19. When a trench excavation uses soldier beams and horizontal sheeting for support, the minimum number of braces for each soldier beam is

    A. 1   B. 2   C. 3   D. 4

19.____

20. Bell and spigot pipe should be laid _____ with the bell end pointed _____.

    A. downstream; upstream   B. downstream; downstream
    C. upstream; upstream   D. upstream; downstream

20.____

21. The specifications state that house sewers should be laid at a grade of not less than 2%. In 40 feet of house sewer, the change in grade for 40 feet should be most nearly _____ inches.

    A. 8   B. 8 1/2   C. 9   D. 9 1/2

21.____

22. Two percent grade on a house sewer is equal to most nearly _____ inch per foot.

    A. 1/8 B. 3/16 C. 1/4 D. 5/16

23. When working underground in spaces that are closed and confined, such as manholes, the gas that is dangerous and most likely of the following to be present is

    A. carbon monoxide
    B. carbon dioxide
    C. ammonia
    D. methane

24. Of the following, air entrained cement would most likely be used in

    A. concrete roadways
    B. precast concrete pipe
    C. precast concrete manholes
    D. the cradle for precast concrete pipe

25. A slump cone is filled to overflowing in _____ layer(s).

    A. one
    B. two separate
    C. three separate
    D. four separate

KEY (CORRECT ANSWERS)

1. B		11. A	
2. A		12. D	
3. D		13. B	
4. B		14. A	
5. B		15. C	
6. D		16. B	
7. B		17. C	
8. C		18. D	
9. A		19. B	
10. C		20. C	

21. D
22. C
23. D
24. A
25. C

EXAMINATION SECTION
TEST 1

DIRECTIONS: Each question or incomplete statement is followed by several suggested answers or completions. Select the one that BEST answers the question or completes the statement. *PRINT THE LETTER OF THE CORRECT ANSWER IN THE SPACE AT THE RIGHT.*

1. In pouring concrete for a large footing, the vibrator is used to move concrete into place. This is

    A. *good* practice as it moves the concrete quickly into place
    B. *good* practice as it eliminates air pockets
    C. *poor* practice as it promotes segregation
    D. *poor* practice as it increases pressure against the forms

    1.____

2. For successful winter work in placing ordinary concrete, adequate protection against the cold should be provided.
Special protection is NOT required when the temperature is over _____ and is required when the temperature is below _____.

    A. 50° F; 50° F
    B. 40° F; 40° F
    C. 30° F; 30° F
    D. 20° F; 20° F

    2.____

3. The MAIN reason for curing concrete is to

    A. prevent segregation of the concrete
    B. prevent the formation of air pockets in the concrete
    C. keep the concrete surface moist
    D. minimize bleeding in the poured concrete

    3.____

4. Of the following, the concrete mix that uses the greatest amount of cement per cubic yard of concrete is

    A. 1:2:4   B. 1:2:3 1/2   C. 1:2 1/2:5   D. 1:2 1/2:3 1/2

    4.____

5. The volume of concrete in a sidewalk 6 ft. x 30 ft. x 4 inches is, in cubic feet, MOST NEARLY

    A. 45   B. 50   C. 55   D. 60

    5.____

6. Of the following, the chemical compound that is added to a concrete mix to accelerate setting in cold weather is

    A. potassium chloride
    B. calcium chloride
    C. sodium nitrate
    D. calcium nitrate

    6.____

7. The compressive strength of concrete

    A. reaches a maximum after 28 days
    B. reaches a maximum after 90 days
    C. reaches a maximum after 180 days
    D. increases after 180 days

    7.____

8. The smallest size of coarse aggregate for concrete is, in inches, MOST NEARLY

   A. 1/4   B. 3/8   C. 1/2   D. 5/8

9. Of the following, the most practical way to determine that the water used in a concrete mix is satisfactory is

   A. send a sample to the laboratory
   B. taste the water
   C. the water is also used for drinking
   D. take a sample and let it stand for a while; and if no sediment at the bottom of the sample, it is satisfactory

10. Grout is

    A. cement, sand with water added so that it will flow readily
    B. cement with water added so that it is fluid
    C. cement and lime with water added so that it will flow readily
    D. gravel, sand, and lime with water added so that it will flow readily

11. Wire fabric has a designation 4 x 12 6/10. Of the following, the statement that is correct is the _____ center to enter and are _____.

    A. longitudinal wires are 12"; 10 gage
    B. longitudinal wires are 4"; 6 gage
    C. transverse wires are 4"; 6 gage
    D. transverse wires are 12; 6 gage

12. The volume of a bag of cement is _____ cubic foot(feet).

    A. 1   B. 1 1/2   C. 2   D. 2 1/2

13. The specifications state: *Forms for slabs shall be set with a camber of 1/4 inch for each 10 feet of span.* The purpose of this requirement is to

    A. compensate for deflection
    B. allow for small errors in setting the formwork
    C. allow for shrinkage of the concrete
    D. compensate for settlement of the supports for the formwork

14. When an inspector goes out to inspect the reinforcing steel before placing of the concrete, the most important drawings he should have with him are the _____ drawings.

    A. structural steel   B. reinforcing steel detail
    C. formwork   D. erection

15. A reinforcing bar has hooks at each end as shown at the right. The detail drawing of the bar will show dimension

    A. A
    B. B
    C. C
    D. D

16. Concrete sidewalks are usually finished with a

    A. screed   B. steel float
    C. wood float   D. darby

17. A new manhole consists of a concrete base made with ordinary cement and a brick superstructure. The minimum time that is usually required after the pouring of the concrete base to start the brickwork is _____ hours.

    A. 24   B. 48   C. 72   D. 96

18. In a new manhole, the slump in the concrete used in the base should be _____ inches.

    A. 2 to 3   B. 3 to 4   C. 4 to 5   D. 5 to 6

19. The dimensions of a cylinder used for testing the strength of concrete is _____ inch diameter and _____ inches high.

    A. 6; 9   B. 6; 12   C. 8; 9   D. 8; 12

20. The specification for the mixing time required for a concrete mix in a Ready-Mix truck is one minute for a one cubic yard batch and a quarter of a minute for every additional cubic yard. The minimum mixing time for a ten cubic yard batch is _____ minutes.

    A. 2 3/4   B. 3   C. 3 1/4   D. 3 1/2

21. The subgrade for a concrete footing is wetted down before concrete is poured into the footing.
    This is

    A. *poor* practice as the water-cement ratio of the concrete will be increased
    B. *poor* practice as it will leave a pocket on the underside of the footing
    C. *good* practice as the water-cement ratio of the concrete will be decreased
    D. *good* practice as the soil will not withdraw water from the concrete

22. Concrete should not be poured too rapidly into the formwork for thin walls primarily because

    A. segregation will result
    B. air pockets will form in the wall
    C. there will be excessive pressure on the formwork
    D. there will be seepage of water through the formwork.

23. The FIRST step in finishing the surface of a concrete pavement is

    A. darbying   B. floating   C. screeding   D. tamping

24. The grade of a reinforcing steel is 40. The 40 represents the _____ of the steel.

    A. tensile strength   B. ultimate strength
    C. yield point   D. elastic limit

25. In reinforced concrete work, stirrups would MOST likely be found in

    A. beams   B. columns   C. walls   D. footings

KEY (CORRECT ANSWERS)

1.	C	11.	B
2.	B	12.	A
3.	C	13.	A
4.	B	14.	B
5.	D	15.	D
6.	B	16.	C
7.	D	17.	A
8.	B	18.	A
9.	C	19.	B
10.	A	20.	C

21. D
22. C
23. C
24. C
25. A

TEST 2

DIRECTIONS: Each question or incomplete statement is followed by several suggested answers or completions. Select the one that BEST answers the question or completes the statement. *PRINT THE LETTER OF THE CORRECT ANSWER IN THE SPACE AT THE RIGHT.*

Questions 1-6.

DIRECTIONS: Questions 1 through 6, inclusive, refer to the following retaining wall.

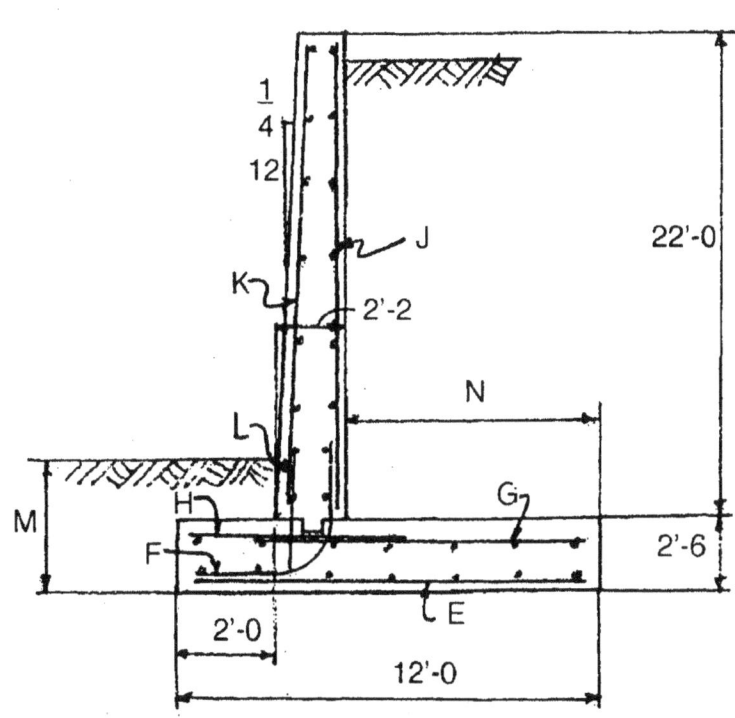

1. The largest size steel bars are most likely to be 1.____
   A. H, K, L   B. E, F, J   C. F, G, H   D. F, G, J

2. Distance M is USUALLY at least 2.____
   A. 2'6"   B. 3'0"   C. 3'6"   D. 4'0"

3. Dimension N is 3.____
   A. 7'6"   B. 7'8"   C. 7'10"   D. 8'0"

4. The width of the wall at the top of the wall is 4.____
   A. 1'8"   B. 1'8 1/2"   C. 1'9"   D. 1'9 1/2"

5. The volume of one foot of wall, in cubic feet, is most nearly (neglect the key at the bottom of the wall) 5.____
   A. 41.2   B. 41.7   C. 42.2   D. 42.6

6. The number of cubic yards of concrete in the footing fifty feet long is, in cubic yards, most nearly (neglect the key at the bottom of the wall)

   A. 54.6   B. 55.6   C. 56.6   D. 57.6

6.___

Questions 7-9.

DIRECTIONS: Questions 7 through 9, inclusive, refer to the markings on a reinforcing bar. The end of a reinforcing bar is marked H6N60.

7. The H in H6N60 indicates the

   A. method of treatment of the reinforcing bar
   B. hardness of the reinforcing steel bar
   C. initial of the steel mill
   D. type of steel in the reinforcing bar

7.___

8. The N in the reinforcing steel bar means

   A. new billet steel
   B. normalized reinforcing steel
   C. the area in which the steel has been produced (north east)
   D. the initial of the manufacturer

8.___

9. The 60 represents the

   A. ultimate strength of the steel
   B. diameter of the steel in millimeters
   C. allowable unit stress in the steel
   D. grade of the steel

9.___

10. The plywood industry produces a special product intended for concrete forming called

    A. structure ply   B. plyform
    C. formply   D. plycoat

10.___

11. Lumber that has been inspected and sorted will carry a grade stamp. The item LEAST likely to be found on the grade stamp is

    A. state of origin   B. grade
    C. species   D. condition of seasoning

11.___

12. In dimensioned lumber, wane indicates

    A. a lack of lumber
    B. narrow annular rings
    C. undersized width or length of lumber
    D. improper seasoning

12.___

13. A sidewalk slab is required to be 4" thick. Measuring down from a nail in the side form that represents the top of the slab, the distance is 4 1/2 inches. Of the following, the BEST action to take is

    A. have the contractor fill the subgrade with a half inch of sand
    B. have the contractor fill the subgrade with a half inch of grout

13.___

C. take no action as the contract requirement is met
D. point out the discrepancy to the contractor and ask him to take appropriate action

14. If high visibility is necessary on the job, a vest _____ colored should be worn. 14._____

   A. red   B. orange   C. yellow   D. green

15. Emulsified asphalt tack coats are preferred to using cut back asphalts PRIMARILY because 15._____

   A. cut-back asphalts present environmental problems
   B. cut-back asphalts are slower drying than emulsified asphalts
   C. cut-back asphalts are faster drying than emulsified asphalts
   D. emulsified asphalts are easier to place than cut-back asphalts

16. Spread footings are footings that 16._____

   A. cover a large area
   B. have an irregular shape
   C. are sometimes called strap footings
   D. transmit their loads through a combination of piles and soil

17. An excavation for a footing is over-excavated and the subgrade is well below the design elevation. Of the following, the BEST action for the contractor to take is 17._____

   A. fill the excavation with well compacted soil until it reaches the design elevation of the bottom of the footing
   B. fill the subgrade with gravel to reach the bottom elevation of the footing
   C. lower the elevation of the footing but retain its thickness
   D. change the footing to a pile supported footing

18. The inspector should be aware of the items in the contract that are unit price so that he can 18._____

   A. make the proper inspection of these items
   B. keep a record of when they are delivered to the job site
   C. make measurements and compute quantities that may be necessary
   D. record the dates of installation of these items

19. The attitudes that an inspector should adopt in dealing with the contractor are to be 19._____

   A. understanding and flexible
   B. helpful and cautious
   C. cautious and skeptical
   D. firm and fair

20. Among the provisions for the safety of workers on the job, the most basic and general one is 20._____

   A. workmen should work slowly
   B. keep alcohol off the job
   C. good housekeeping
   D. wear suitable clothing for extreme weather conditions

21. Ladders should extend a minimum of _____ above the level to which they lead.

   A. six feet
   B. knee-high
   C. waist-high
   D. five feet

22. An inspector notices a worker working in an unsafe manner. Of the following, the BEST action the inspector can take is to

   A. tell the worker the correct way to work
   B. tell the worker's supervisor of the unsafe behavior of the worker
   C. record the incident in your log book
   D. notify the contractor so that the unsafe practice will cease

23. In making the daily report, personal remarks by the inspector should not be included. Of the following, the best reason for this exclusion is

   A. it may raise questions as to the accuracy of the report
   B. the wrong people may read the daily report
   C. the inspector should have no opinions
   D. it may indicate bias on the part of the inspector

24. The major difference between a softwood and a hardwood in forestry terms is

   A. the softwoods are from the south and the hardwoods are from the north
   B. the softwoods are evergreens and the hardwoods are deciduous
   C. the softwoods are soft and the hardwoods are hard
   D. there is one grading method for softwoods and another grading method for hardwoods

25. Lumber is considered unseasoned if it has a moisture content of not less than _____ percent in weight of water.

   A. 17
   B. 20
   C. 23
   D. 26

KEY (CORRECT ANSWERS)

1.	D	11.	A
2.	D	12.	A
3.	C	13.	C
4.	B	14.	B
5.	D	15.	A
6.	B	16.	A
7.	C	17.	A
8.	A	18.	C
9.	D	19.	D
10.	B	20.	C

21. C
22. B
23. D
24. B
25. B

EXAMINATION SECTION
TEST 1

DIRECTIONS: Each question or incomplete statement is followed by several suggested answers or completions. Select the one that BEST answers the question or completes the statement. *PRINT THE LETTER OF THE CORRECT ANSWER IN THE SPACE AT THE RIGHT.*

1. Before placing asphalt block for a pavement on the concrete base, the concrete base should be

    A. wet down with water
    B. painted with hot asphaltic cement
    C. covered with a bitumen-sand bed
    D. covered with broken stone

    1.____

2. Of the following ingredients, the one which is present in asphaltic concrete but not in a sheet asphalt mix is

    A. asphaltic cement   B. sand
    C. mineral dust   D. broken stone

    2.____

3. Of the following materials, the one which would make the BEST macadam base course is

    A. freshly broken rock consisting of angular pieces
    B. broken rock which had weathered for a long time
    C. gravel consisting of smooth round rock
    D. freshly crushed gravel

    3.____

4. The one of the following in which a surface heater would be MOST useful is

    A. new concrete construction
    B. new asphalt construction
    C. repair work on concrete
    D. repair work on asphalt

    4.____

5. A pneumatic jack hammer is powered by

    A. compressed air   B. electricity
    C. steam   D. water pressure

    5.____

6. A mattock could be BEST used in place of a

    A. hammer   B. pick-axe   C. rake   D. shovel

    6.____

7. The one of the following tools that is used to finish concrete so that a very smooth surface is obtained is

    A. template   B. trowel
    C. vibrator   D. wooden float

    7.____

8. The type of cement used in MOST concrete work is called

    A. asbestos   B. natural   C. Portland   D. rock

    8.____

29

9. Cement brought on the job in bags should be

   A. piled in criss-cross stacks on the ground near the work
   B. piled in stacks 10 bags high in a convenient place on the ground
   C. put on a platform and covered with waterproof covering
   D. put under a tree or awning where the sun's rays can't reach it

10. In the concrete trade, sand is called

    A. binder
    B. coarse aggregate
    C. filler
    D. fine aggregate

11. A 1:2:4 concrete mix means one part _____, two parts _____, four parts _____.

    A. cement; gravel; sand
    B. cement; sand; gravel
    C. gravel; sand; cement
    D. sand; gravel; cement

12. A slump test is used in concrete to determine

    A. consistency
    B. construction
    C. expansion
    D. slope

13. After mixing, the *initial* set of concrete will take place in about _____ hour(s).

    A. 3/4 of an
    B. 2 1/4
    C. 4 3/4
    D. 8

14. Concrete that has become partly set in the mixer should be

    A. covered with water for about 24 hours to soften it before using
    B. discarded and not used at all
    C. mixed in with another regular batch of concrete before using
    D. re-tempered by adding more cement and mixed again before using

15. In hot weather, newly-placed concrete will set better when it is

    A. covered with wet burlap
    B. dried by exposure to the sun
    C. mixed with grout
    D. shaded from the sun's rays

16. A 1:2:4 concrete mix is prepared on the job with 10 gallons of water. This concrete mix is

    A. *desirable,* because it will require less tamping
    B. *desirable,* because it will set faster
    C. *undesirable,* because its strength is reduced by excess water
    D. *undesirable,* because it will show less honeycomb

17. Of the following, the one which will lengthen the setting time of concrete is a(n)

    A. higher water temperature
    B. increase in proportion of water used
    C. less humid atmosphere
    D. shorter mixing period

18. Of the following, quick drying of concrete will MOST likely cause 18.____

    A. air bubbles   B. bumps
    C. cracks   D. swelling

19. Of the following, the BEST way to prepare an old concrete surface for a new layer of concrete is to 19.____

    A. clean it and apply a rich cement mortar
    B. cover it with wet sand
    C. steam and dry it
    D. wash it thoroughly and leave it wet

20. Grout is used MAINLY to 20.____

    A. fill surface impressions and imperfections
    B. lower the freezing point of the concrete mix
    C. make the base harden faster
    D. provide a wearing surface layer

21. The usual method of repairing cracks in concrete roadways is to fill with 21.____

    A. limestone   B. mineral filler
    C. sand   D. tar

22. Joints are placed in concrete sidewalks to take care of 22.____

    A. bumps   B. cracks
    C. drainage   D. expansion and contraction

23. To take care of surface drainage, concrete sidewalks usually have slopes of _____ inch(es) to the foot. 23.____

    A. 1/4   B. 1   C. 2   D. 3

24. The grade of a street is the 24.____

    A. AAA rating of the street's riding qualities
    B. difference in height between the crown and berm
    C. slope of a cut or fill
    D. variation in elevation per 100 feet

25. If a street rises 2' in 400', the grade is 25.____

    A. 0.2%   B. 0.5%   C. 2.0%   D. 5.0%

KEY (CORRECT ANSWERS)

1. C
2. D
3. A
4. D
5. A

6. B
7. B
8. C
9. C
10. D

11. B
12. A
13. A
14. B
15. A

16. C
17. B
18. C
19. A
20. A

21. D
22. D
23. A
24. D
25. B

TEST 2

DIRECTIONS: Each question or incomplete statement is followed by several suggested answers or completions. Select the one that BEST answers the question or completes the statement. *PRINT THE LETTER OF THE CORRECT ANSWER IN THE SPACE AT THE RIGHT.*

1. The top course of an asphalt pavement is known as the _____ course. 1._____

    A. aggregate   B. base   C. binder   D. wearing

2. In paving terms, a two-course concrete sidewalk is one which is 2._____

    A. composed of concrete both hand and machine mixed
    B. composed of two layers, a base and a wearing surface
    C. wide enough for traffic going in opposite directions
    D. wide enough for two pedestrians to walk side by side

3. The foundations for asphalt surface should be 3._____

    A. clean and damp
    B. clean and dry
    C. damp and sprinkled with sand
    D. dry and sprinkled with sand

4. A catch basin is used to 4._____

    A. detain floating rubbish which might clog a sewer
    B. hold water used in flushing sewers
    C. record and measure the depth of flow of sewage
    D. regulate the flow of sewage to a treatment plant

5. A sewer built to carry the flows in excess of the capacity of an existing sewer is called a _____ sewer. 5._____

    A. lateral   B. main   C. relief   D. trunk

6. A sewer designed to carry domestic sewage, industrial waste, and storm sewage is called a 6._____

    A. combined sewer   B. house connection
    C. sanitary sewer   D. storm sewer

7. A pipe conveying sewage from a single building to a common sewer is called a 7._____

    A. catch basin   B. grease trap
    C. house connection   D. relief sewer

8. The PRINCIPAL effort in maintaining sewers is to keep them 8._____

    A. clean and unobstructed
    B. free from poisonous gases
    C. free of illegal connections
    D. properly backfilled

9. Catch basins in unpaved streets should be cleaned

   A. daily in winter, weekly in summer
   B. once a year
   C. every six months
   D. after every large storm

10. In using a flexible sewer rod to clean a sewer, the work is usually begun at the

    A. chimney between manholes
    B. nearest catch basin
    C. top of the flooded manhole
    D. nearest house connection

11. In flushing sewers, the MOST important of the following qualities of the water used is its

    A. cleanliness B. quantity
    C. temperature D. velocity

12. Grease can be prevented from entering a sewer by the

    A. addition of copper sulfate
    B. installation of a copper ring in pipe joints
    C. installation of a separator
    D. coating of the outside of the pipe with tar

13. Manholes are used CHIEFLY as a(n)

    A. access for cleaning sewers
    B. outlet for sewer gas
    C. run-off for storm water
    D. support for sewer pipes

14. If the sewage at a manhole is backed up, it indicates MOST probably that, with respect to this manhole, there is an obstruction in the

    A. nearest catch basin B. nearest house connection
    C. upstream sewer D. downstream sewer

15. The one of the following at which a manhole in a sewer line is NOT necessary is wherever there is a

    A. change in direction
    B. change in pipe size
    C. considerable change in grade
    D. house connection

16. Manholes are usually placed at intervals of _____ to _____ feet.

    A. 50; 75 B. 100; 200 C. 700; 900 D. 1200; 1400

17. Of the following, the STRONGEST method for sheeting a trench is

    A. box sheeting B. poling boards
    C. stay bracing D. vertical sheeting

18. The one of the following that would be MOST commonly used to join a house sewer to a common sewer is a(n)

    A. increaser
    B. reducer
    C. running trap
    D. Y branch

19. After making joints in sewer pipe, the minimum safe length of time to allow before they should be exposed to running water is _____ hour(s).

    A. 1
    B. 8
    C. 24
    D. 48

20. The one of the following that is the LEAST important health precaution for a sewer worker to take is

    A. frequent washing
    B. shading his eyes from reflected light
    C. using an antiseptic in cuts
    D. wearing rubber gloves

Questions 21-25.

DIRECTIONS: Column I below contains pictures of pipe connections used in sewer lines. Column II lists the names of these fittings. For each picture, indicate the capital letter preceding its correct name in Column II.

21.

COLUMN II
A. Elbow
B. Reducer
C. Running trap
D. T branch
E. Y branch

22.

23.

4 (#2)

24. 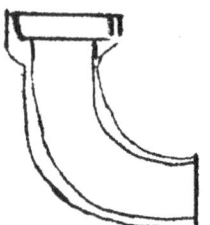   24.___

25. 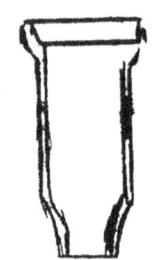   25.___

KEY (CORRECT ANSWERS)

1. D   11. D
2. B   12. C
3. B   13. A
4. A   14. D
5. C   15. D

6. A   16. A
7. C   17. D
8. A   18. D
9. D   19. C
10. C   20. B

21. E
22. D
23. C
24. A
25. B

EXAMINATION SECTION
TEST 1

DIRECTIONS: Each question consists of a statement. You are to indicate whether the statement is TRUE (T) or FALSE (F). *PRINT THE LETTER OF THE CORRECT ANSWER IN THE SPACE AT THE RIGHT.*

1. A stillson wrench may properly be used on wrought iron pipe.   1.____

2. A pneumatic hammer is run by electricity.   2.____

3. A pneumatic drill, when not in use, should be left standing on its rod.   3.____

4. A cubic yard contains 27 cubic feet.   4.____

5. A tarpaulin is a lubricating oil for air compressors.   5.____

6. In working in manholes or pits, it is advisable to have one or two of the crew outside in case of emergency.   6.____

7. Men should be cautioned against entering manholes or vaults without first testing the air inside.   7.____

8. An air compressor is best used to yarn a joint.   8.____

9. To dig a trench, it is best to use a square-pointed shovel.   9.____

10. A street or road which rises at a uniform grade of 5 feet in 100 feet has a 5% grade.   10.____

11. If a candle will burn at the bottom of a manhole, it is a sign of gas and men should keep out.   11.____

12. It is good practice to wait until a sewer has been ventilated before going down into it.   12.____

13. It is good practice to drop lighted matches down a manhole to see if gas is present.   13.____

14. Workmen handling tar or asphalt should have their trousers fastened tightly around their ankles.   14.____

15. Cement brought to a job in bags should be piled neatly in criss-cross stacks on the ground.   15.____

16. Bagged cement should be piled about 25 bags high.   16.____

17. Men placing cement and concrete should have sleeves rolled up since they can work faster that way.   17.____

18. When mixing concrete, workmen should not stand so the wind blows in their faces.   18.____

19. Manholes are provided at suitable intervals along a sewer so that it may be inspected and cleaned.   19.____

20. The operator of a pneumatic drill should grasp it very loosely to prevent fatigue from constant vibration.   20.____

21. A catch basin's main use is to prevent storm water from entering a combined sewer. 21.___

22. Catch basins are generally built of brick or concrete. 22.___

23. Catch basins in New York City are generally cleaned by the use of orange peel type buckets. 23.___

24. A flexible rod is a tool often used in cleaning sewers. 24.___

25. Sewer obstructions can be removed by running scrapers and brushes through the sewer pipe. 25.___

KEY (CORRECT ANSWERS)

1.	T	11.	F
2.	F	12.	T
3.	F	13.	F
4.	T	14.	T
5.	F	15.	F
6.	T	16.	F
7.	T	17.	F
8.	F	18.	T
9.	F	19.	T
10.	T	20.	F

21.	F
22.	T
23.	T
24.	T
25.	T

TEST 2

DIRECTIONS: Each question consists of a statement. You are to indicate whether the statement is TRUE (T) or FALSE (F). *PRINT THE LETTER OF THE CORRECT ANSWER IN THE SPACE AT THE RIGHT.*

1. In flushing sewers, the amount of water used is more important than the speed at which the water is played into the sewer. 1.____
2. Many pavement failures can be traced to the action of water or moisture. 2.____
3. A pot hole in paving is a device for heating tar. 3.____
4. A surface heater is usually used to heat the binder course. 4.____
5. Tampers are used to compact a pavement in places where rollers cannot reach. 5.____
6. A straight edge is used to determine the smoothness of a finished pavement. 6.____
7. Concrete is a mixture of cement, sand, gravel and water in the proper proportions. 7.____
8. To clean a concrete mixer, you should operate it with water and small stones in the drum. 8.____
9. A concrete mixture will do a satisfactory job if it is allowed to stand one hour before placing. 9.____
10. Rapid drying of concrete adds to its strength. 10.____
11. In mixing concrete, the quantity of water used makes no difference. 11.____
12. Cracks in concrete open wider in cold weather. 12.____
13. A 1:2:4 concrete mix means one part cement, two parts sand, and four parts gravel. 13.____
14. Coarse aggregate consists of clean crushed rock or gravel. 14.____
15. A good way to prevent concrete from sticking to forms is to wet the forms with oil. 15.____
16. Concrete that has partly set in the mixer can be broken up and used with another batch of concrete. 16.____
17. Wings of a roadway are at the same elevation as center line. 17.____
18. The crown of a street is the fall from the center to edges. 18.____
19. A cold patch mixture when ready to be deposited usually contains wire mesh. 19.____
20. Grout is used to fill cracks in asphalt pavement. 20.____
21. In pouring cracks, just enough material should be used to fill the opening. 21.____
22. In hot weather, a pavement will contract. 22.____
23. Streets should usually be patched with the same material used in their construction. 23.____

24. Expansion joints are used in paving to provide for changes in temperature. 24.___

25. The main purpose of a seal coat in paving is to water-proof a surface. 25.___

KEY (CORRECT ANSWERS)

1.	F	11.	F
2.	T	12.	T
3.	F	13.	T
4.	F	14.	T
5.	T	15.	T
6.	T	16.	F
7.	T	17.	F
8.	T	18.	T
9.	F	19.	F
10.	F	20.	F

21. T
22. F
23. T
24. T
25. T

EXAMINATION SECTION
TEST 1

DIRECTIONS: Each question or incomplete statement is followed by several suggested answers or completions. Select the one that BEST answers the question or completes the statement. *PRINT THE LETTER OF THE CORRECT ANSWER IN THE SPACE AT THE RIGHT.*

1. When filling an empty aqueduct, the valve should be opened

    A. slowly to prevent damage to the aqueduct
    B. rapidly to fill the line as soon as possible
    C. slowly to prevent rapid lowering of the reservoir level
    D. rapidly so that there are no air locks

2. The BEST way of detecting the location of a suspected chlorine leak is by placing a _____ near the suspected leak.

    A. rag, which has been dipped in a strong ammonia water,
    B. match
    C. piece of litmus paper
    D. flow meter

3. The term *run-off* refers to the

    A. amount a valve must be turned in order to open it fully
    B. length of time an electric motor continues to turn after the current is shut off
    C. amount of rainfall which flows from the ground surface into the streams and reservoirs
    D. distance the water falls from the intake gate to the turbine

4. Algae in reservoirs may be killed by using

    A. zeolite   B. copper sulphate
    C. sodium chloride   D. calcium chloride

5. The one of the following types of valves that USUALLY operates without manual control is a(n) _____ valve.

    A. check   B. globe   C. gate   D. angle

6. Rate of flow of water through a water treatment plant is USUALLY referred to in terms of

    A. c.f.s.   B. c.f.m.   C. r.p.m.   D. m.g.d.

7. In order to make it easier to operate a large valve or gate, pressures on both sides of the valve or gate are balanced by

    A. using weights on each side of the valve or gate
    B. opening a smaller by-pass valve
    C. partially shutting down the water in the upstream line
    D. opening the downstream valve very slowly

8. Leaves are removed from the water entering the treatment plant or aqueduct by

    A. skimming   B. coagulating   C. draining   D. screening

9. Odors, due to gases in the water, are removed by

   A. surging   B. sluicing   C. aerating   D. clarifying

10. Chlorine residual refers to the

   A. amount of chlorine that must be added to the water
   B. amount of chlorine that remains in the water after a given period
   C. method of adding the chlorine to the water
   D. method of protecting personnel using chlorine from the effects of the chlorine

11. One of the processes that takes place in an Imhoff tank is

   A. oxidation   B. flocculation   C. digestion   D. coagulation

12. As used in a sewage disposal plant, *effluent* refers to the

   A. basic treatment process of sewage
   B. time it takes for complete treatment of sewage
   C. type of control the plant uses for treatment
   D. final liquid coming out of the treatment process

13. A grit chamber operates on the basis that

   A. grit will settle out of slow-moving water
   B. grit will float and can be removed by skimming the surface
   C. increasing the rate of flow of water will leave the grit behind
   D. spraying water into the air will cause the heavier grit to separate from the water

14. The purpose of sedimentation in any sewage treatment process is to

   A. aerate the sewage
   B. increase the chlorine content of the sewage
   C. remove suspended matter from the sewage
   D. kill the bacteria in the sewage

15. The final treatment for sludge before it is disposed of is

   A. drying   B. adding chlorine
   C. mixing   D. washing

16. The amount of sewage applied to a filter bed is GENERALLY controlled by a

   A. sluice gate   B. flow meter
   C. dosing siphon   D. regulating valve

17. Methane gas which results from the sewage treatment process is MOST frequently

   A. vented to the outside air to prevent injury to plant personnel
   B. used as a fuel in the plant
   C. combined with other gases to render it harmless
   D. burned in the open air

18. The filtering material in a *filter bed* at a sewage treat-ment plant is USUALLY

   A. activated charcoal   B. sand
   C. alum   D. ammonium chloride

19. Cleaning sewer lines is USUALLY done by the use of a

    A. catch basin B. flushometer
    C. sewer rod D. center line

20. One of the ways of locating a leak in a water line is by using a

    A. manometer B. sounding rod
    C. poling board D. diffusor

21. MOST sewer pipes are made of

    A. cast iron B. agricultural tile
    C. brass D. copper

22. One of the materials generally used in caulking joints in bell and spigot pipe is

    A. tar B. litharge C. red lead D. oakum

23. Water pipe must be laid at least two feet below the ground surface MAINLY to

    A. prevent freezing
    B. discourage malicious tampering
    C. reduce the pressure required to make the water flow
    D. eliminate possibility of damage to roads in case of water main break

24. When soldering copper gutters, the flux that is GENERALLY used is

    A. sal ammoniac B. resin
    C. killed muriatic acid D. calcium chloride

25. A good concrete mix for use in the foundations of a small building is

    A. 1:2:5 B. 5:2:1 C. 2:5:1 D. 1:5:2

26. When painting steel, red lead is used MAINLY as a

    A. primer coat so final coat will adhere better
    B. primer coat to protect the steel from rusting
    C. finish coat to protect the steel from the action of the sun and water
    D. second coat to bind the primer and finish coats

27. Studs in frame buildings are USUALLY

    A. 1" x 4" B. 1" x 6" C. 2" x 4" D. 2" x 6"

28. A cement mortar used in brickwork is USUALLY made more workable by adding

    A. phosphate B. lime C. calcium D. grout

Questions 29-32.

DIRECTIONS: The following four questions numbered 29 to 32, inclusive, are to be answered in accordance with the rules of the department of water supply, gas and electricity.

29. The term *water course* refers to

   A. aqueducts only
   B. pipe lines only
   C. natural or artificial streams only
   D. all of the above

30. Where a swimming pool discharges upon or into the ground and the water is not treated, the minimum distance between such discharge and a stream MUST be at least _____ feet.

   A. 50 B. 100 C. 250 D. 450

31. According to the above rules, clothes may

   A. be washed in a spring, if the spring does not feed directly into a reservoir
   B. be washed in a spring if the place where this is being done is at least one mile from a reservoir
   C. be washed in a spring provided a chlorinated soap is used
   D. not be washed in a spring

32. Industrial wastes may

   A. be discharged into a stream provided the stream does not feed directly into a reservoir
   B. be discharged into a stream, provided the point of discharge is at least one mile from a reservoir
   C. be discharged into a stream if the wastes are purified in an approved manner
   D. not be discharged into a stream

33. One method of determining the height of the water in a stream feeding into a reservoir is by means of a

   A. venturi meter
   B. flow meter
   C. hook gage
   D. strain gage

34. When digging a deep trench, the sides are USUALLY prevented from caving in by using

   A. shoulders B. blocking C. pins D. sheathing

35. The FIRST precaution a worker should take before entering a sewer manhole is to

   A. put on hard-toed shoes
   B. put on safety goggles
   C. check that the next manhole upstream is not obstructed
   D. test the air in the manhole

36. Assume that a fuse blows upon connecting a light load to the circuit. You replace it with the same size fuse, and again the fuse blows.
    The BEST thing to do in this case is to

   A. connect a wire across the fuse so it cannot blow under such a light load
   B. replace the fuse with one having a higher rating
   C. check the wiring of the circuit
   D. place two fuses in series to prevent blowing

37. Of the following material, the one that is BEST for fill as a subgrade for a road is   37.____

    A. sand
    B. silt
    C. clay
    D. a mixture of sand, silt, and clay

38. When dealing with leaking chlorine, it is IMPORTANT to remember that chlorine is   38.____

    A. highly flammable
    B. made safe by spraying water on it
    C. not corrosive
    D. heavier than air

39. Cast iron pipe is MOST frequently cut with a(n)   39.____

    A. hack saw
    B. diamond point chisel
    C. burning torch
    D. abrasive wheel

40. Water hammer in a pipe line is BEST reduced by installing   40.____

    A. a pressure regulator
    B. an air chamber
    C. smaller pipes and valves
    D. larger pipes and valves

KEY (CORRECT ANSWERS)

1. A	11. C	21. A	31. D
2. A	12. D	22. D	32. D
3. C	13. A	23. A	33. C
4. B	14. C	24. C	34. D
5. A	15. A	25. A	35. D
6. D	16. C	26. B	36. C
7. B	17. B	27. C	37. D
8. D	18. B	28. B	38. D
9. C	19. C	29. D	39. B
10. B	20. B	30. B	40. B

TEST 2

DIRECTIONS: Each question or incomplete statement is followed by several suggested answers or completions. Select the one that BEST answers the question or completes the statement. *PRINT THE LETTER OF THE CORRECT ANSWER IN SPACE AT THE RIGHT.*

1. When used in conjunction with a centrifugal pump, a foot valve

    A. equalizes the pressure on both sides of the pump
    B. regulates the amount of water flowing through the pump
    C. prevents water in the pump from flowing back down the suction line
    D. adjusts the speed of the pump to the amount of water to be pumped

2. Grounding an electric motor is

    A. *good* practice because the motor will operate better
    B. *poor* practice because the motor will not operate as well
    C. *good* practice because it protects against shock hazards
    D. *poor* practice because it increases shock hazards

3. The one of the following wrenches that should NOT be used to turn a nut is a wrench.

    A. monkey   B. box   C. stillson   D. socket

4. A drill is GENERALLY removed from the chuck of a portable electric drill by using a

    A. drift pin   B. wedge
    C. centerpunch   D. key

5. The finished surface of a dirt road is MOST frequently maintained with a

    A. blade grader   B. bulldozer
    C. dragline   D. carryall

6. Frequent stalling of a truck engine is MOST probably due to a

    A. weak battery   B. low battery water level
    C. leaking oil filter D. dirty carburetor

7. If the reading of the oil pressure gage on a gasoline motor should suddenly drop to zero, the FIRST thing the operator should do is to

    A. check the filter
    B. inspect the oil lines
    C. tighten the oil pan bolts
    D. stop the motor

8. A tractor is to be stored for two months. In order to keep it in BEST condition, it should be

    A. drained of all fuel and oil
    B. lubricated every week
    C. started up periodically and run until warm
    D. steam cleaned and all water drained from the radiator

9. Trees suffering from transplanting shock are quickly helped by

A. deep watering   B. foliage feeding
C. root feeding   D. vitamin treatments

10. For MOST rapid healing, trees should be pruned during

    A. November, December, and January
    B. February, March, and April
    C. May, June, and July
    D. August, September, and October

11. The blades of a lawn mower should be set so that the blades

    A. firmly touch the bed knife
    B. barely touch the bed knife
    C. clear the bed knife by 1/16 inch
    D. clear the bed knife by 1/8 inch

12. The MAIN reason for mulching is to

    A. fertilize the soil
    B. prevent erosion
    C. protect plants from the cold
    D. kill insects

13. A compost heap would MOST likely include

    A. lawn clippings   B. sand
    C. stumps of trees   D. gravel

14. Of the following statements with regard to *seeding,* the one that is CORRECT is:

    A. Seeds should be sown on a windy day
    B. The ground should be watered heavily after seeding
    C. Seeding should be done primarily on a bright and sunny day
    D. It is not necessary to carefully apportion the amount of seeds sown

15. Organic matter is often added to soil to better condition it for growing plants.
    Of the following, the item that is NOT organic matter is

    A. lime   B. peat   C. manure   D. leaf mold

16. Of the following, the BEST way to store coniferous seedlings which cannot be planted for a few days is to

    A. unwrap them and put them in a dark, dry location
    B. place them flat on the ground in a sunny location so they can get plenty of light and air
    C. place them in a trench dug in the earth and cover the root ends with soil
    D. make sure the ball is not loosened and keep in a hothouse

17. Transplanting of seedlings is BEST done in early

    A. spring   B. summer   C. autumn   D. winter

3 (#2)

18. After planting privet hedges, they are frequently cut back to within a few inches of the ground.
    This is USUALLY done to

    A. remove dead parts of the hedge
    B. insure dense growth from the ground up
    C. speed up root development
    D. reduce the possibility of insect damage while the hedge is taking root

19. *Heaving* of pavements in wintertime is USUALLY caused by the

    A. difference of expansion of pavement and subgrade
    B. freezing of water in subgrade
    C. loss of bond between pavement and subgrade
    D. brittleness of pavement

20. Erosion of side slopes caused by the action of water is GREATEST when the soil is

    A. silt   B. clay   C. hardpan   D. silty-clay

21. The MAIN reason for making a crown in a road pavement is to

    A. reduce the amount of paving material necessary
    B. make it easier for cars to go around a curve
    C. drain surface water
    D. increase the strength of the pavement where it is most needed

22. The MAIN reason for paving ditches at the side of a road is to

    A. prevent damage from cars
    B. permit the ditch to carry more water
    C. prevent erosion of the soil in the ditch
    D. block water from getting under the pavement

23. Assume that vitrified clay tile pipe, with open joints, is being used as the underdrain for a roadway.
    This pipe should be laid

    A. directly on the bottom of the trench
    B. on a bed of clay
    C. on a bed of peat
    D. on a bed of gravel

24. A macadam road is one in which the base is GENERALLY made of

    A. asphalt   B. broken stone
    C. concrete   D. stabilized soil

25. To loosen compacted rocky earth road surfaces, the BEST piece of equipment to use is a

    A. disc harrow   B. drag line   C. bulldozer   D. scarifier

26. Oiling of an earth road is BEST done

    A. in the winter before the snow falls
    B. when you expect much rain

C. in the spring during dry weather
D. immediately after snow is cleared from the road

27. Cracks in concrete roads are BEST repaired by filling them with

   A. tar   B. grout
   C. mineral filler D. sand

28. When repairing patches in old asphalt pavements, the edges of the patch should FIRST be painted with

   A. the same material used for the patch
   B. kerosene
   C. asphalt cement
   D. asphalt binder

29. The sum of 3 1/4, 5 1/8, 2 1/2, and 3 3/8 is

   A. 14   B. 14 1/8   C. 14 1/4   D. 14 3/8

30. Assume that it takes 6 men 8 days to do a particular job.
    If you have only 4 men available to do this job and they all work at the same speed, then the number of days it would take to complete the job would be

   A. 11   B. 12   C. 13   D. 14

31. The city aims to supply *potable* water. As used in this sentence, the word *potable* means MOST NEARLY

   A. clear   B. drinkable   C. fresh   D. adequate

32. Water, after being purified, should not be turbid. As used in this sentence, the word turbid means MOST NEARLY

   A. cloudy   B. warm   C. infected   D. hard

33. The flow of water is *impeded* by the silt in the bottom of the stream.
    As used in this sentence, the word *impeded* means MOST NEARLY

   A. dammed   B. hindered   C. helped   D. dirtied

Questions 34-35.

DIRECTIONS: Questions 34 and 35 are based on the following paragraph.

Repeated burning of the same area should be avoided. Burning should not be done on impervious, shallow, unstable, or highly erodible soils, or on steep slopes - especially in areas subject to heavy rains or rapid snowmelt. When existing vegetation is likely to be killed or seriously weakened by the fire, measures should be taken to assure prompt revegetation of the burned area. Burns should be limited to relatively small proportions of a watershed unit so that the stream channels will be able to carry any increased flows with a minimum of damage.

34. According to the above paragraph, planned burning should be limited to small areas of the watershed because

    A. the fire can be better controlled
    B. existing vegetation will be less likely to be killed
    C. plants will grow quicker in small areas
    D. there will be less likelihood of damaging floods

35. According to the above paragraph, burning usually should be done on soils that

    A. readily absorb moisture
    B. have been burnt before
    C. exist as a thin layer over rock
    D. can be flooded by nearby streams

36. If a foreman does not understand the instructions that are given to him by the district engineer, the BEST thing to do is to

    A. work out the solution to the problem himself
    B. do the job in the way he thinks is best
    C. get one of the other foremen to do the job
    D. ask that the instructions be repeated and clarified

37. The BEST foreman is the one who

    A. can work as fast as the fastest man in the crew
    B. is the most skilled mechanic
    C. can get the most work out of the men
    D. is the strongest man

38. Complimenting a man for good work is

    A. *good* practice since it will give the man an incentive to continue working well
    B. *poor* practice because the other men will become jealous
    C. *good* practice because in the future the foreman will not have to supervise this man
    D. *poor* practice since the man should work well without needing compliments

39. In dealing with his men, it is MOST important that a foreman be

    A. a disciplinarian   B. stern
    C. fair   D. chummy with his men

40. When issuing a violation to a member of the public, it is MOST important that a foreman be

    A. aloof and refuse to discuss the violation
    B. stern, and warn the person to correct the violation immediately
    C. courteous and explain what must be done to correct the violation
    D. friendly and volunteer assistance to correct the violation

KEY (CORRECT ANSWERS)

1. C	11. B	21. C	31. B
2. C	12. C	22. C	32. A
3. C	13. A	23. D	33. B
4. D	14. B	24. B	34. D
5. A	15. A	25. D	35. A
6. D	16. C	26. C	36. D
7. D	17. A	27. A	37. C
8. C	18. B	28. C	38. A
9. B	19. B	29. C	39. C
10. B	20. A	30. B	40. C

WORK SCHEDULING

EXAMINATION SECTION
TEST 1

DIRECTIONS: Each question or incomplete statement is followed by several suggested answers or completions. Select the one that BEST answers the question or completes the statement. *PRINT THE LETTER OF THE CORRECT ANSWER IN THE SPACE AT THE RIGHT.*

Questions 1-6.

DIRECTIONS: Questions 1 through 6 are to be answered SOLELY on the basis of the information given in the ELEVATOR OPERATORS' WORK SCHEDULE shown below.

ELEVATOR OPERATORS' WORK SCHEDULE				
Operator	Hours of Work	A.M. Relief Period	Lunch Hour	P.M. Relief Period
Anderson	8:30-4:30	10:20-10:30	12:00-1:00	2:20-2:30
Carter	8:00-4:00	10:10-10:20	11:45-12:45	2:30-2:40
Daniels	9:00-5:00	10:20-10:30	12:30-1:30	3:15-3:25
Grand	9:30-5:30	11:30-11:40	1:00-2:00	4:05-4:15
Jones	7:45-3:45	9:45-9:55	11:30-12:30	2:05-2:15
Lewis	9:45-5:45	11:40-11:50	1:15-2:15	4:20-4:30
Nance	8:45-4:45	10:50-11:00	12:30-1:30	3:05-3:15
Perkins	8:00-4:00	10:00-10:10	12:00-1:00	2:40-2:50
Russo	7:45-3:45	9:30-9:40	11:30-12:30	2:10-2:20
Smith	9:45-5:45	11:45-11:55	1:15-2:15	4:05-4:15

1. The two operators who are on P.M. relief at the SAME time are   1.____

    A. Anderson and Daniels B. Carter and Perkins
    C. Jones and Russo   D. Grand and Smith

2. Of the following, the two operators who have the SAME lunch hour are   2.____

    A. Anderson and Perkins B. Daniels and Russo
    C. Grand and Smith   D. Nance and Russo

3. At 12:15, the number of operators on their lunch hour is   3.____

    A. 3   B. 4   C. 5   D. 6

4. The operator who has an A.M. relief period right after Perkins and a P.M. relief period right before Perkins is   4.____

    A. Russo   B. Nance   C. Daniels   D. Carter

5. The number of operators who are scheduled to be working at 4:40 is   5.____

    A. 5   B. 6   C. 7   D. 8

53

6. According to the schedule, it is MOST correct to say that 6.____
   A. no operator has a relief period during the time that another operator has a lunch hour
   B. each operator has to wait an identical amount of time between the end of lunch and the beginning of P.M. relief period
   C. no operator has a relief period before 9:45 or after 4:00
   D. each operator is allowed a total of 1 hour and 20 minutes for lunch hour and relief periods

---

KEY (CORRECT ANSWERS)

1. D
2. A
3. C
4. D
5. A
6. D

TEST 2

DIRECTIONS: Each question or incomplete statement is followed by several suggested answers or completions. Select the one that BEST answers the question or completes the statement. *PRINT THE LETTER OF THE CORRECT ANSWER IN THE SPACE AT THE RIGHT.*

Questions 1-7.

DIRECTIONS: Questions 1 through 7 are to be answered SOLELY on the basis of the time sheet and instructions given below.

The following time sheet indicates the times that seven laundry workers arrived and left each day for the week of August 23. The times they arrived for work are shown under the heading IN, and the times they left are shown under the heading OUT. The letter (P) indicates time which was used for personal business. Time used for this purpose is charged to annual leave. Lunch time is one-half hour from noon to 12:30 P.M. and is not accounted for on this time record.

The employees on this shift are scheduled to work from 8:00 A.M. to 4:00 P.M. Lateness is charged to annual leave. Reporting after 8:00 A.M. is considered late.

	MON.		TUES.		WED.		THURS.		FRI.	
	AM IN	PM OUT	AM IN	PM OUT	AM IN	PM OUT	AM IN	PM OUT	AM IN	PM OUT
Baxter	7:50	4:01	7:49	4:07	8:00	4:07	8:20	4:00	7:42	4:03
Gardner	8:02	4:00	8:20	4:00	8:05	3:30(P)	8:00	4:03	8:00	4:07
Clements	8:00	4:04	8:03	4:01	7:59	4:00	7:54	4:06	7:59	4:00
Tompkins	7:56	4:00	Annual leave		8:00	4:07	7:59	4:00	8:00	4:01
Wagner	8:04	4:03	7:40	4:00	7:53	4:04	8:00	4:09	7:53	4:00
Patterson	8:00	2:30(P)	8:15	4:04	Sick leave		7:45	4:00	7:59	4:04
Cunningham	7:43	4:02	7:50	4:00	7:59	4:02	8:00	4:10	8:00	4:00

1. Which one of the following laundry workers did NOT have any time charged to annual leave or sick leave during the week?   1.____

    A. Gardner   B. Clements   C. Tompkins   D. Cunningham

2. On which day did ALL the laundry workers arrive on time?   2.____

    A. Monday   B. Wednesday   C. Thursday   D. Friday

3. Which of the following laundry workers used time to take care of personal business?   3.____

    A. Baxter and Clements   B. Patterson and Cunningham
    C. Gardner and Patterson   D. Wagner and Tompkins

4. How many laundry workers were late on Monday?   4.____

    A. 1   B. 2   C. 3   D. 4

5. Which one of the following laundry workers arrived late on three of the five days?   5.____

    A. Baxter   B. Gardner   C. Wagner   D. Patterson

55

6. The percentage of laundry workers reporting to work late on Tuesday is MOST NEARLY 6.___
   A. 15%   B. 25%   C. 45%   D. 50%

7. The percentage of laundry workers that were absent for an entire day during the week is MOST NEARLY 7.___
   A. 6%   B. 9%   C. 15%   D. 30%

KEY (CORRECT ANSWERS)

1. D
2. D
3. C
4. B
5. B
6. C
7. D

TEST 3

Questions 1-9.

DIRECTIONS: Questions 1 through 9 are to be answered SOLELY on the basis of the following information and timesheet given below.

The following is a foreman's timesheet for his crew for one week. The hours worked each day or the reason the man was off on that day are shown on the sheet. *R* means rest day. *A* means annual leave. *S* means sick leave. Where a man worked only part of a day, both the number of hours worked and the number of hours taken off are entered. The reason for absence is entered in parentheses next to the number of hours taken off.

Name	Saturday	Sunday	Monday	Tuesday	Wednesday	Thursday	Friday
Smith	R	R	7	7	7	3 4(A)	7
Jones	R	7	7	7	7	7	R
Green	R	R	7	7	S	S	S
White	R	R	7	7	A	7	7
Doe	7	7	7	7	7	R	R
Brown	R	R	A	7	7	7	7
Black	R	R	S	7	7	7	7
Reed	R	R	7	7	7	7	S
Roe	R	R	A	7	7	7	7
Lane	7	R	R	7	7	A	S

1. The caretaker who worked EXACTLY 21 hours during the week is

   A. Lane   B. Roe   C. Smith   D. White

2. The TOTAL number of hours worked by all caretakers during the week is

   A. 268   B. 276   C. 280   D. 288

3. The two days of the week on which MOST caretakers were off are

   A. Thursday and Friday   B. Friday and Saturday
   C. Saturday and Sunday   D. Sunday and Monday

4. The day on which three caretakers were off on sick leave is

   A. Monday   B. Friday   C. Saturday   D. Sunday

5. The two workers who took LEAST time off during the week are

   A. Doe and Reed   B. Jones and Doe
   C. Reed and Smith   D. Smith and Jones

6. The caretaker who worked the LEAST number of hours during the week is

   A. Brown   B. Green   C. Lane   D. Roe

7. The caretakers who did NOT work on Thursday are

   A. Doe, White, and Smith
   B. Green, Doe, and Lane
   C. Green, Doe, and Smith
   D. Green, Lane, and Smith

8. The day on which one caretaker worked ONLY 3 hours is 8._____
   A. Friday   B. Saturday   C. Thursday   D. Wednesday

9. The day on which ALL caretakers worked is 9._____
   A. Monday   B. Thursday   C. Tuesday   D. Wednesday

KEY (CORRECT ANSWERS)

1. A
2. B
3. C
4. B
5. B

6. B
7. B
8. C
9. C

TEST 4

Questions 1-6.

DIRECTIONS: Questions 1 through 6 are to be answered SOLELY on the basis of the table below which shows the initial requests made by staff for vacation. It is to be used with the RULES AND GUIDELINES to make the decisions and judgments called for in each of the questions.

VACATION REQUESTS FOR THE ONE YEAR PERIOD FROM MAY 1, YEAR X THROUGH APRIL 30, YEAR Y				
Name	Work Assignment	Date Appointed	Accumulated Annual Leave Days	Vacation Periods Requested
DeMarco	MVO	Mar. 2003	25	May 3-21; Oct. 25-Nov. 5
Moore	Dispatcher	Dec. 1997	32	May 24-June 4; July 12-16
Kingston	MVO	Apr. 2007	28	May 24-June 11; Feb. 7-25
Green	MVO	June 2006	26	June 7-18; Sept. 6-24
Robinson	MVO	July 2008	30	June 28-July 9; Nov. 15-26
Reilly	MVO	Oct. 2009	23	July 5-9; Jan. 31-Mar. 3
Stevens	MVO	Sept. 1996	31	July 5-23; Oct. 4-29
Costello	MVO	Sept. 1998	31	July 5-30; Oct. 4-22
Maloney	Dispatcher	Aug. 1992	35	July 5-Aug. 6; Nov. 1-5
Hughes	Director	Feb. 1990	38	July 26-Sept. 3
Lord	MVO	Jan. 2010	20	Aug. 9-27; Feb. 7-25
Diaz	MVO	Dec. 2009	28	Aug. 9-Sept. 10
Krimsky	MVO	May 2006	22	Oct. 18-22; Nov. 22-Dec. 10

RULES AND GUIDELINES

1. The two Dispatchers cannot be on vacation at the same time, nor can a Dispatcher be on vacation at the same time as the Director.

2. For the period June 1 through September 30, not more than three MVO's can be on vacation at the same time.

3. For the period October 1 through May 31, not more than two MVO's at a time can be on vacation.

4. In cases where the same vacation time is requested by too many employees for all of them to be given the time under the rules, the requests of those who have worked the longest will be granted.

5. No employee may take more leave days than the number of annual leave days accumulated and shown in the table.

6. All vacation periods shown in the table and described in the questions below begin on a Monday and end on a Friday.

7. Employees work a five-day week (Monday through Friday). They are off weekends and holidays with no charges to leave balances. When a holiday falls on a Saturday or Sunday, employees are given the following Monday off without charge to annual leave.

2 (#4)

8. Holidays:
   May 31 October 25 January 1
   July 4 November 2 February 12
   September 6 November 25 February 21
   October 11 December 25 February 21

9. An employee shall be given any part of his initial requests that is permissible under the above rules and shall have first right to it despite any further adjustment of schedule.

---

1. Until adjustments in the vacation schedule can be made, the vacation dates that can be approved for Krimsky are

   A. Oct. 18-22; Nov. 22-Dec. 10
   B. Oct. 18-22; Nov. 29-Dec. 10
   C. Oct. 18-22 *only*
   D. Nov. 22-Dec. 10 *only*

2. Until adjustments in the vacation schedule can be made, the vacation dates that can be approved for Maloney are

   A. July 5-Aug. 6; Nov. 1-5
   B. July 5-23; Nov. 1-5
   C. July 5-9; Nov. 1-5
   D. Nov. 1-5 *only*

3. According to the table, Lord wants a vacation in August and another in February. Until adjustments in the vacation schedule can be made, he can be allowed to take _____ of the August vacation and _____ of the February vacation.

   A. all; none
   B. all; almost half
   C. almost all; almost half
   D. almost half; all

4. Costello cannot be given all the vacation he has requested because

   A. the MVO's who have more seniority than he has have requested time he wishes
   B. he does not have enough accumulated annual leave
   C. a dispatcher is applying for vacation at the same time as Costello
   D. there are five people who want vacation in July

5. According to the table, how many leave days will DeMarco be charged for his vacation from October 25 through November 5?

   A. 10   B. 9   C. 8   D. 7

6. How many leave days will Moore use if he uses the requested vacation allowable to him under the rules?

   A. 9   B. 10   C. 14   D. 15

KEY (CORRECT ANSWERS)

1. D
2. B
3. A
4. B
5. C
6. A

TEST 5

Questions 1-8.

DIRECTIONS: Questions 1 through 8 are to be answered SOLELY on the basis of Charts I, II, III, and IV. Assume that you are the supervisor of Operators R, S, T, U, V, W, and X, and it is your responsibility to schedule their lunch hours.

The charts each represent a possible scheduling of lunch hours during a lunch period from 11:30 - 2:00. An operator-hour is one hour of time spent by one operator. Each box on the chart represents one half-hour. The boxes marked L represent the time when each operator is scheduled to have her lunch hour. For example, in Chart I, next to Operator R, the boxes for 11:30 - 12:00 and 12:00 -12:30 are marked L. This means that Operator R is scheduled to have her lunch hour from 11:30 to 12:30.

I

	11:30-12:00	12:00-12:30	12:30-1:00	1:00-1:30	1:30-2:00
R	L	L			
S		L	L		
T		L	L		
U			L	L	
V			L	L	
W				L	L
X				L	L

II

	11:30-12:00	12:00-12:30	12:30-1:00	1:00-1:30	1:30-2:00
R				L	L
S		L	L		
T	L	L			
U		L	L		
V				L	L
W				L	L
X		L	L		

III

	11:30-12:00	12:00-12:30	12:30-1:00	1:00-1:30	1:30-2:00
R	L	L			
S				L	L
T	L	L			
U			L	L	
V	L	L			
W			L	L	
X			L	L	

IV

	11:30-12:00	12:00-12:30	12:30-1:00	1:00-1:30	1:30-2:00
R	L	L			
S	L	L			
T		L	L		
U			L	L	
V				L	L
W				L	L
X			L	L	

1. If, under the schedule represented in Chart II, Operator R has her lunch hour changed to 12:30-1:30, that leaves how many operator-hours of phone coverage from 1:00-2:00? 1.___

   A. 2 B. 2 1/2 C. 3 D. 4 1/2

2. If Operator S asks you whether she and Operator T may have the same lunch hour, you could accommodate her by using the schedule in Chart 2.___

   A. I B. II C. III D. IV

3. From past experience you know that the part of the lunch period when the phones are busiest is from 12:30-1:30. Which chart shows the BEST phone coverage from 12:30 to 1:30? 3.___

   A. I B. II C. III D. IV

4. At least three operators have the same lunch hour according to Chart(s) 4.___

   A. II and III
   B. II and IV
   C. III only
   D. IV only

62

5. Which chart would provide the POOREST phone coverage during the period 12:00-1:30, based on total number of operator-hours from 12:00 to 1:30?

   A. I B. II C. III D. IV

6. Which chart would make it possible for U, W, and X to have the same lunch hour?

   A. I B. II C. III D. IV

7. The portion of the lunch period during which the telephones are least busy is 11:30-12:30.
   Which chart is MOST likely to have been designed with that fact in mind?

   A. I B. II C. III D. IV

8. Assume that you have decided to use Chart IV to schedule your operators' lunch hours on a specific day. Operator T asks you if she can have her lunch hour changed to 1:00-2:00.
   If you grant her request, how many operators will be working during the period 12:00 to 12:30?

   A. 1 B. 2 C. 4 D. 5

KEY (CORRECT ANSWERS)

1. D
2. A
3. B
4. A
5. A

6. C
7. C
8. D

TEST 6

Questions 1-13.

DIRECTIONS: Questions 1 through 13 consist of a statement. You are to indicate whether the statement is TRUE (T) or FALSE (F). *PRINT THE LETTER OF THE CORRECT ANSWER IN THE SPACE AT THE RIGHT.* Questions 1 through 13 are to be answered SOLELY on the basis of the information given in the table below.

DEPARTMENT OF FERRIES ATTENDANTS WORK ASSIGNMENT - JULY 2003					
Name	Year Employed	Ferry Assigned	Hours of Work	Lunch Period	Days Off
Adams	1999	Hudson	7 AM - 3 PM	11-12	Fri. and Sat.
Baker	1992	Monroe	7 AM - 3 PM	11-12	Sun. and Mon.
Gunn	1995	Troy	8 AM - 4 PM	12-1	Fri. and Sat.
Hahn	1989	Erie	9 AM - 5 PM	1-2	Sat. and Sun.
King	1998	Albany	7 AM - 3 PM	11-12	Sun. and Mon.
Nash	1993	Hudson	11 AM - 7 PM	3-4	Sun. and Mon.
Olive	2003	Fulton	10 AM - 6 PM	2-3	Sat. and Sun.
Queen	2002	Albany	11 AM - 7 PM	3-4	Fri. and Sat.
Rose	1990	Troy	11 AM - 7 PM	3-4	Sun. and Mon.
Smith	1991	Monroe	10 AM - 6 PM	2-3	Fri. and Sat.

1. The chart shows that there are only five (5) ferries being used. 1.___

2. The attendant who has been working the LONGEST time is Rose. 2.___

3. The Troy has one more attendant assigned to it than the Erie. 3.___

4. Two (2) attendants are assigned to work from 10 P.M. to 6 A.M. 4.___

5. According to the chart, no more than one attendant was hired in any year. 5.___

6. The NEWEST employee is Olive. 6.___

7. There are as many attendants on the 7 to 3 shift as on the 11 to 7 shift. 7.___

8. MOST of the attendants have their lunch either between 12 and 1 or 2 and 3. 8.___

9. All the employees work four (4) hours before they go to lunch. 9.___

10. On the Hudson, Adams goes to lunch when Nash reports to work. 10.___

11. All the attendants who work on the 7 to 3 shift are off on Saturday and Sunday. 11.___

12. All the attendants have either a Saturday or Sunday as one of their days off. 12.___

13. At least two (2) attendants are assigned to each ferry. 13.___

KEY (CORRECT ANSWERS)

1. F	6. T	11. F
2. F	7. T	12. T
3. T	8. F	13. F
4. F	9. T	
5. T	10. T	

EXAMINATION SECTION
TEST 1

DIRECTIONS: Each question or incomplete statement is followed by several suggested answers or completions. Select the one that BEST answers the question or completes the statement. *PRINT THE LETTER OF THE CORRECT ANSWER IN THE SPACE AT THE RIGHT.*

1. When all of her employees are assigned to perform identical routine tasks, a supervisor would PROBABLY find it most difficult to differentiate among these employees as to the
    A. amount of work each completed
    B. initiative each one shows in doing the work
    C. number of errors in each one's work
    D. number of times each one is absent or late

1._____

2. The one of the following guiding principles to which a supervisor should give the GREATEST weight when it becomes necessary to discipline an employee is that the
    A. discipline should be of such a nature as to improve the future work of the employee
    B. main benefit gained in disciplining one employee is that all employees are kept from breaking the same rule
    C. morale of all the employees should be improved by the discipline of the one
    D. rules should be applied in a fixed and unchanging manner

2._____

3. In using praise to encourage employees to do better work, the supervisor should realize that praising an employee too often is not good MAINLY because the
    A. employee will be resented by her fellow employees
    B. employee will begin to think she's doing too much work
    C. praise will lose its value as an incentive
    D. supervisor doesn't have the time to praise an employee frequently

3._____

4. A supervisor notices that one of her best employees has apparently begun to loaf on the job.
   In this situation, the supervisor should FIRST
    A. allow the employee a period of grace in view of her excellent record
    B. change the employee's job assignment
    C. determine the reason for the change in the employee's behavior
    D. take disciplinary action immediately as she would with any other employee

4._____

5. A supervisor who wants to get a spirit of friendly cooperation from the employees in her unit is MOST likely to be successful if she
    A. makes no exceptions in strictly enforcing department procedures
    B. shows a cooperative spirit herself
    C. tells them they are the best in the department
    D. treats them to coffee once in a while

5._____

6. *Accidents do not just happen.*
   In view of this statement, it is important for the supervisor to realize that
   A. accidents are sometimes deliberate
   B. combinations of unavoidable circumstances cause accidents
   C. she must take the blame for each accident
   D. she should train her employees in accident prevention

7. Suppose your superior points out to you several jobs that were poorly done by the employees under your supervision.
   As the supervisor of these employees, you should
   A. accept responsibility for the poor work and take steps to improve the work in the future
   B. blame the employees for shirking on the job while you were busy on other work
   C. defend the employees since up to this time they were all good workers
   D. explain that the poor work was due to circumstances beyond your control

8. If a supervisor discovers a situation which is a possible source of grievance, it would be BEST for her to
   A. be ready to answer the employees when they make a direct complaint
   B. do nothing until the employees make a direct complaint
   C. tell the employees, in order to keep them from making a direct complaint, that nothing can be done
   D. try to remove the cause before the employees make a direct complaint

9. Suppose there is a departmental rule that requires supervisors to prepare reports of unusual incidents by the end of the tour of duty in which the incident occurs.
   The MAIN reason for requiring such prompt reporting is that
   A. a quick decision can be made whether the employee involved was neglectful of her duty
   B. other required reports cannot be made out until this one is turned in
   C. the facts are recorded before they are forgotten or confused by those involved in the incident
   D. the report is submitted before the supervisor required to make the report may possibly leave the department

10. A good practical method to use in determining whether an employee is doing his job properly is to
    A. assume that if he asks no questions, he knows the work
    B. question him directly on details of the job
    C. inspect and follow-up the work which is assigned to him
    D. ask other employees how this employee is making out

11. If an employee continually asks how he should do his work, you should
    A. dismiss him immediately
    B. pretend you do not hear him unless he persists
    C. explain the work carefully but encourage him to use his own judgment
    D. tell him not to ask so many questions

12. You have instructed an employee to complete a job in a certain area.
To be sure that the employee understands the instructions you have given him, you should
    A. ask him to repeat the instructions to you
    B. check with him after he has done the job
    C. watch him while he is doing the job
    D. repeat the instructions to the employee

13. One of your men disagrees with your evaluation of his work.
Of the following, the BEST way to handle this situation would be to
    A. explain that you are in a better position to evaluate his work than he is
    B. tell him that since other men are satisfied with your evaluation, he should accept their opinions
    C. explain the basis of your evaluation and discuss it with him
    D. refuse to discuss his complaint in order to maintain discipline

14. Of the following, the on which is NOT a quality of leadership desirable in a supervisor is
    A. intelligence   B. integrity   C. forcefulness   D. partiality

15. Of the following, the one which LEAST characterizes the grapevine is that it
    A. consists of a tremendous amount of rumor, conjecture, information, advice, prediction, and even orders.
    B. seems to rise spontaneously, is largely anonymous, spreads rapidly, and changes in unpredictable directions
    C. can be eliminated without any great effort
    D. commonly fills the gaps left by the regular organizational channels of communication

16. When a superintendent delegates authority to a foreman, of the following, it would be MOST advisable for the superintendent to
    A. set wide limits of such authority to allow the foreman considerable leeway
    B. define fairly closely the limits of the authority delegated to the foreman
    C. wait until the foreman has some experience in the assignment before setting limits to his authority
    D. inform him that it is the foreman's ultimate basic responsibility to get the work done

17. One of the hallmarks of a good supervisor is his ability to use many different methods of obtaining information about the status of work in progress.
Which one of the following would probably indicate that a supervisor does NOT have this ability?
    A. Holding specified staff meetings at specified intervals
    B. Circulating among his subordinates as often as possible
    C. Holding staff meetings only when absolutely necessary
    D. Asking subordinates to come in and discuss the progress of their work and their problems

18. Of the following, the one which is the LEAST important factor in deciding that additional training is necessary for the men you supervise is that
    A. the quality of work is below standard
    B. supplies are being wasted
    C. too much time is required to do specific jobs
    D. the absentee rate has declined

19. To promote proper safety practices in the operation of power tools and equipment, you should emphasize in meetings with the staff that
    A. every accident can be prevented through proper safety regulations
    B. proper safety practices will probably make future safety meetings unnecessary
    C. when safety rules are followed, tools and equipment will work better
    D. safety rules are based on past experience with the best methods of preventing accidents

20. Employee morale is the way employees feel about each other and their job. To a supervisor, it should be a sign of good morale if the employees
    A. are late for work
    B. complain about their work
    C. willingly do difficult jobs
    D. take a long time to do simple jobs

21. A supervisor who encourages his workers to make suggestions about job improvement shows his workers that he
    A. is not smart enough to improve the job himself
    B. wants them to take part in making improvements
    C. does not take the job seriously
    D. is not a good supervisor

22. Suppose that your supervisor tells you that a procedure which has been followed for years is going to be changed. It is your job to make sure the workers you supervises understand and accept the new procedure.
    What would be the BEST thing for you to do in this situation?
    A. Give a copy of the new procedure to each worker with orders that it must be followed
    B. Explain the new procedure to one worker and have him explain it to the others
    C. Ask your supervisor to explain the new procedure since he has more authority
    D. call your workers together to explain and discuss the new procedure

23. One of the foundations of scientific management of an organization is the proper use of control measures.
    Of the following, the BEST way, in general, to implement control measures is to
    A. develop suitable procedures, systems, and guidelines for the organization
    B. evaluate the actual employees' job performance realistically and reasonably
    C. set standards which are designed to increase productivity
    D. publish a set of rules and insist upon strict compliance with these rules

24. A district superintendent would MOST likely be justified in taking up a matter with his borough superintendent when the problem involved
    A. a dispute among different factions in his district
    B. a section foreman's difficulties with his assistant foreman
    C. his own men and others not under his control
    D. methods of doing the work and the amount of production

25. The superintendent has the authority to recommend disciplinary action. He can BEST use this authority to
    A. demonstrate his authority as a superintendent
    B. improve a man's work
    C. make it less difficult for other superintendents to maintain order
    D. punish the men for wrong-doing

KEY (CORRECT ANSWERS)

1.	B	11.	C
2.	A	12.	A
3.	C	13.	C
4.	C	14.	D
5.	B	15.	C
6.	D	16.	B
7.	A	17.	C
8.	D	18.	D
9.	C	19.	D
10.	C	20.	C

21.	B
22.	D
23.	C
24.	B
25.	B

TEST 2

DIRECTIONS: Each question or incomplete statement is followed by several suggested answers or completions. Select the one that BEST answers the question or completes the statement. *PRINT THE LETTER OF THE CORRECT ANSWER IN THE SPACE AT THE RIGHT.*

1. From the standpoint of equal opportunity, the MOST critical item that a superintendent should focus on is
   A. assigning only minority workers to supervisory positions
   B. helping minority employees to upgrade their knowledge so they may qualify for higher positions
   C. placing minority workers in job categories above their present level of ability so that they can *sink or swim*
   D. disregarding merit system principles

   1.____

2. After careful deliberation, you have decided that one of your workers should be disciplined.
   It is MOST important that the
   A. discipline be severe for best results
   B. discipline be delayed as long as possible
   C. worker understands why he is being disciplined
   D. other workers be consulted before the discipline is administered

   2.____

3. Of the following, the MOST important qualities of an employee chosen for a supervisory position are
   A. education and intelligence
   B. interest in the objectives and activities of the agency
   C. skill in performing the type of work to be supervised
   D. knowledge of the work and leadership ability

   3.____

4. Of the following, the CHIEF characteristic which distinguishes a good supervisor from a poor supervisor is the good supervisor's
   A. ability to favorably impress others
   B. unwillingness to accept monotony or routine
   C. ability to deal constructively with problem situations
   D. strong drive to overcome opposition

   4.____

5. Of the following, the MAIN disadvantage of on-the-job training is that, generally,
   A. special equipment may be needed
   B. production may be slowed down
   C. the instructor must maintain an individual relationship with the trainee
   D. the on-the-job instructor must be better qualified than the classroom instructor

   5.____

6. If it becomes necessary for you, as a supervisor, to give a subordinate employee confidential information, the MOST effective of the following steps to take is to make sure the information is kept confidential by the employee is to

   6.____

2 (#2)

    A. tell the employee that the information is confidential and is not to be repeated
    B. threaten the employee with disciplinary action if the information is repeated
    C. offer the employee a merit increase as an incentive for keeping the information confidential
    D. remind the employee at least twice a day that the information is confidential and is not to be repeated

7. Three new men have just been assigned to work under your supervision. Every time you give them an assignment, one of these men asks you several questions.
Of the following, the MOST desirable action for you to take is to
    A. assure him of your confidence in his ability to carry out the assignment correctly without asking so many questions
    B. have all three men listen to your answers to these questions
    C. point out that the other two men do the job without asking so many questions
    D. tell him to see if he can get the answers from other workers before coming to you

7.____

8. Two of your subordinates suggest that you recommend a third man for an above-standard service rating because of his superior work.
You should
    A. ask the two subordinates whether the third man knows that they intended to discuss this matter with you
    B. explain to the two subordinates that an above-standard service rating for one man would have a detrimental effect on many of the other men
    C. recommend the man for an above-standard service rating if there is sufficient justification for it
    D. tell the two subordinates that the matter of service ratings is not their concern

8.____

9. All of the following are indications of good employee morale EXCEPT
    A. the number of grievances are lowered
    B. labor turnover is decreased
    C. the amount of supervision required is lowered
    D. levels of production are lowered

9.____

10. All of the following statements regarding the issuance of direct orders are true EXCEPT
    A. use direct orders only when necessary
    B. make sure that the receiver of the direct order is qualified to carry out the order
    C. issue direct orders in clear, concise words
    D. give direct orders only in writing

10.____

11. In order to achieve the BEST results in on-the-job training, supervisors should
    A. allow frequent coffee breaks during the training period
    B. be in a higher salary range than that of the individuals they are training
    C. have had instructions or experience in conducting such training
    D. have had a minimum of five years' experience in the job

    11._____

12. Of the following, the LEAST important quality of a good supervisor is
    A. technical competence
    B. teaching ability
    C. ability to communicate with others
    D. ability to socialize with subordinates

    12._____

13. One of your usually very hard working, reliable employees brings in a bottle of whiskey to celebrate his birthday during the rest period.
    Which one of the following actions should you take?
    A. Offer to pay for the cost of the whiskey
    B. Confiscate the bottle
    C. Tell him to celebrate after working hours
    D. Pretend that you have not seen the bottle of whiskey

    13._____

14. Assume that you find it necessary to discipline two subordinates, Mr. Tate and Mr. Sawyer, for coming to work late on several occasions. Their latenesses have had disruptive effects on the work schedule, and you have given both of them several verbal warnings. Mr. Tate has been in your work unit for many years, and his work has always been satisfactory. Mr. Sawyer is a probationary employee, who has had some problem in learning your procedures. You decide to give Mr. Tate one more warning, in private, for his latenesses.
    According to good supervisory practice, which one of the following disciplinary actions should you take with regard to Mr. Sawyer?
    A. Give him a reprimand in front of his co-workers, to make a lasting impression
    B. Recommend dismissal since he has not yet completed his probationary period
    C. Give him one more warning, in private, for his latenesses
    D. Recommend a short suspension or payroll deduction to impress upon him the importance of coming to work on time

    14._____

15. Assume that you have delegated a very important work assignment to Johnson, one of your most experienced subordinates. Prior to completion of the assignment, your superior accidentally discovers that the assignment is being carried out incorrectly, and tells you about it.
    Which one of the following responses is MOST appropriate for you to give to your superior?
    A. *I take full responsibility, and I will see to it that the assignment is carried out correctly.*
    B. *Johnson has been with us for many years now and should know better.*

    15._____

C. *It really isn't Johnson's fault, rather it is the fault of the ancient equipment we have to do the job.*
D. *I think you should inform Johnson since he is the one at fault, not I.*

16. Assume that you observe that one of your employees is talking excessively with other employees, quitting early, and taking unusually long rest periods. Despite these abuses, she is one of your most productive employees, and her work is usually of the highest quality.
    Of the following, the MOST appropriate action to take with regard to this employee is to
    A. ignore these infractions since she is one of your best workers
    B. ask your superior to reprimand her so that you can remain on the employee's good side
    C. reprimand her since not doing so would lower the morale of the other employees
    D. ask another of your subordinates to mention these infractions to the offending employee and suggest that she stop breaking rules

    16.____

17. Assume that you have noticed that an employee whose attendance had been quite satisfactory is now showing marked evidence of a consistent pattern of absences.
    Of the following, the BEST way to cope with this problem is to
    A. wait several weeks to see whether this pattern continues
    B. meet with the employee to try to find out the reasons for this change
    C. call a staff meeting and discuss the need for good attendance
    D. write a carefully worded warning to the employee

    17.____

18. It is generally agreed that the successful supervisor must know how to wisely delegate work to her subordinates since she cannot do everything herself.
    Which one of the following practices is MOST likely to result in ineffective delegation by a supervisor?
    A. Establishment of broad controls to assure feedback about any deviations from plans
    B. Willingness to let subordinates use their own ideas about how to get the job done, where appropriate
    C. Constant observance of employees to see if they are making any mistakes
    D. Granting of enough authority to make possible the accomplishment of the delegated work

    18.____

19. Suppose that, in accordance with grievance procedures, an employee brings a complaint to you, his immediate supervisor.
    In dealing with his complaint, the one of the following which is MOST important for you to do is to
    A. talk to the employee's co-workers to learn whether the complaint is justified
    B. calm the employee by assuring him that you will look into the matter as soon as possible

    19.____

C. tell your immediate superior about the employee's complaint
D. give the employee an opportunity to tell the full story

20. Holding staff meetings at regular intervals is generally considered to be a good supervisory practice.
Which one of the following subjects is LEAST desirable for discussion at such a meeting?
    A. Revisions in agency personnel policies
    B. Violation of an agency rule by one of the employees present
    C. Problems of waste and breakage in the work area
    D. Complaints of employees about working conditions

21. Suppose that you are informed that your staff is soon to be reduced by one-third due to budget problems.
Which one of the following steps would be LEAST advisable in your effort to maintain a quality service with the smaller number of employees?
    A. Directing employees to speed up operations
    B. Giving employees training or retraining
    C. Rearranging the work area
    D. Revising work methods

22. Of the following which action on the part of the supervisor LEAST likely to contribute to upgrading the skills of her subordinates?
    A. Providing appropriate training to subordinates
    B. Making periodic evaluations of subordinates and discussing the evaluations with the subordinates
    C. Consistently assigning subordinates to those tasks with which they are familiar
    D. Giving increased responsibility to appropriate subordinates

23. Suppose that a new employee on your staff has difficulty in performing his assigned tasks after having been given training.
Of the following courses of action, the one which would be BEST for you, his supervisor, to take FIRST is to
    A. change his work assignment
    B. give him a poor evaluation since he is obviously unable to do the work
    C. give him the training again
    D. have him work with an employee who is more experienced in the tasks for a short while

24. Several times, an employee has reported to work unit for duty because he had been drinking. He refused to get counseling for his emotional problems when this was suggested by his superior. Last week, his supervisor warned him that he would face disciplinary action if he again reported to work unfit for duty because of drinking. Now, the employee has again reported to work in that condition.

Of the following, the BEST action for the supervisor to take now would be to
A. arrange to have the employee transferred to another work location
B. give the employee one more chance by pretending to not notice his condition this time
C. start disciplinary action against the employee
D. warn him that he will face disciplinary action if he reports for work in that condition again

25. An employee has been calling in sick repeatedly, and these absences have disrupted the work schedule.
To try to make sure that the employee use sick leave only on days when he is actually sick, which of the following actions would be the BEST for his supervisor to take?
A. Telephone the employee's home on days when he is out on sick leave
B. Require the employee to obtain a note from a physician explaining the reason for his absence whenever he uses sick leave in the future
C. Require that he get a complete physical examination and have his doctor send a report to the supervisor
D. Warn the employee that he will face disciplinary action the next time he stays out on sick leave

25.____

KEY (CORRECT ANSWERS)

1. B
2. C
3. D
4. C
5. B

6. A
7. B
8. C
9. D
10. D

11. C
12. D
13. C
14. C
15. A

16. C
17. B
18. C
19. D
20. B

21. A
22. C
23. D
24. C
25. B

TEST 3

DIRECTIONS: Each question or incomplete statement is followed by several suggested answers or completions. Select the one that BEST answers the question or completes the statement. *PRINT THE LETTER OF THE CORRECT ANSWER IN THE SPACE AT THE RIGHT.*

1. Suppose that, as a supervisor, you have an idea for changing the way a certain task is performed by your staff so that it will be less tedious and get done faster. Of the following, the MOST advisable action for you to take regarding this idea is to
   A. issue a written memorandum explaining the new method and giving reasons why it is to replace the old one
   B. discuss it with your staff to get their reactions and suggestions
   C. set up a training class in the new method for your staff
   D. try it out on an experimental basis on half the staff

   1.____

2. A troubled subordinate privately approaches his supervisor in order to talk about a problem on the job.
   In this situation, the one of the following actions that is NOT desirable on the part of the supervisor is to
   A. ask the subordinate pertinent questions to help develop points further
   B. close his office door during the talk to block noisy distractions
   C. allow sufficient time to complete the discussion with the subordinate
   D. take over the conversation so the employee won't be embarrassed

   2.____

3. Suppose that one of your goals as a supervisor is to foster good working relationships between yourself and your employees, without undermining your supervisory effectiveness by being too friendly.
   Of the following, the BEST way to achieve this goal when dealing with employees' work problems is to
   A. discourage individual personal conferences by using regularly scheduled staff meetings to discuss work problems
   B. try to resolve work problems within a relatively short period of time
   C. insist that employees put all work problems into writing before seeing you
   D. maintain an open-door policy, allowing employees complete freedom of access to you without making appointments to discuss work problems

   3.____

4. An employee under your supervision complains that he is assigned to work late more often than any of the other employees. You check the records and find that this isn't so.
   You should
   A. advise this employee not to worry about what the other employees do but to see that he puts in a full day's work himself
   B. explain to this employee that you get the same complaint from all the other employees
   C. inform this employee that you have checked the records and the complaint is not justified
   D. not assign this employee to work late for a few days in order to keep him satisfied

   4.____

5. An employee has reported late for work several times.
   His supervisor should
   A. give this employee less desirable assignments
   B. overlook the lateness if the employee's work is otherwise exceptional
   C. recommend disciplinary action for habitual lateness
   D. talk the matter over with the employee before doing anything further

6. In choosing a man to be in charge in his absence, the supervisor should select FIRST the employee who
   A. has ability to supervise others
   B. has been longest with the organization
   C. has the nicest appearance and manner
   D. is most skilled in his assigned duties

7. An employee under your supervision comes to you to complain about a decision you have made in assigning the men. He is excited and angry. You think what he is complaining about is not important, but it seems very important to him.
   The BEST way for you to handle this is to
   A. let him talk until *he gets it off his chest* and then explain the reasons for your decision
   B. refuse to talk to him until he has cooled off
   C. show him at once how unimportant the matter is and how ridiculous his arguments are
   D. tell him to take it up with your superior if he disagrees with your decision

8. Suppose that a new employee has been appointed and assigned to your supervision.
   When this man reports for work, it would be BEST for you to
   A. ask him questions about different problems connected with his line of work and see if he answers them correctly
   B. check him carefully while he carries out some routine assignment that you give him
   C. explain to him the general nature of the work he will be required to do
   D. make a careful study of his previous work record before coming to your department

9. *The competent supervisor will be friendly with the employees under his supervision but will avoid close familiarity.*
   This statement is justified MAINLY because
   A. a friendly attitude on the part of the supervisor toward the employee is likely to cause suspicion on the part of the employee
   B. a supervisor can handle his employees better if he doesn't know their personal problems
   C. close familiarity may interfere with the discipline needed for good supervisor-subordinate relationships
   D. familiarity with the employees may be a sign of lack of ability on the part of the supervisor

10. An employee disagrees with the instructions that you, his supervisor, have given him for carrying out a certain assignment.
    The BEST action for you to take is to tell this employee that
    A. he can do what he wants but you will hold him responsible for failure
    B. orders must be carried out or morale will fall apart
    C. this job has been done in this way for many years with great success
    D. you will be glad to listen to his objections and to his suggestions for improvement

11. As a supervisor, it is LEAST important for you to use a new employee's probationary period for the purpose of
    A. carefully checking how he performs the work you assign him
    B. determining whether he can perform the duties of his job efficiently
    C. preparing him for promotion to a higher position
    D. showing him how to carry out his assigned duties properly

12. Suppose you have just given an employee under your supervision instructions on how to carry out a certain assignment.
    The BEST way to check that he has understood your instructions is to
    A. ask him to repeat your instructions word for word
    B. check the progress of his work the first chance you get
    C. invite him to ask questions if he has any doubts
    D. question him briefly about the main points of the assignment

13. Suppose you find it necessary to change a procedure that the men under your supervision have been following for a long time.
    A good way to get their cooperation for this change would be to
    A. bring them together to talk over the new procedure and explain the reasons for its adoption
    B. explain to the men that if most of them still don't approve of the change after giving it a fair try you will consider giving it up
    C. give them a few weeks' notice of the proposed change in procedure
    D. not enforce the new procedure strictly at the beginning

14. An order can be given by a supervisor in such a way as to make the employee want to obey it.
    According to this statement, it is MOST reasonable to suppose that
    A. a person will be glad to obey an order if he realizes that he must
    B. if an order is given properly, it will be obeyed more willingly
    C. it is easier to obey an order than to give one correctly
    D. supervisors should inspire confidence by their actions as well as by their words

15. If one of the men you supervise disagrees with how you rate his work, the BEST way for you to handle this is to
    A. advise him to appeal to your superior about it
    B. decline to discuss the matter with him in order to keep discipline
    C. explain why you rate him the way you do and talk it over with him
    D. tell him that you are better qualified to rate his work than he is

16. A supervisor should be familiar with the experience and abilities of the employees under his supervision MAINLY because
    A. each employee's work is highly important and requires a person of outstanding ability
    B. it will help him to know which employees are best fitted for certain assignments
    C. nearly all men have the same basic ability to do any job equally well
    D. superior background shortly shows itself in superior work quality, regardless of assignment

16.____

17. The competent supervisor will try to develop respect rather than fear in his subordinates.
    This statement is justified MAINLY because
    A. fear is always present and, for best results, respect must be developed to offset it
    B. it is generally easier to develop respect in the men than it is to develop fear
    C. men who respect their supervisor are more likely to give more than the required minimum amount and quality of work
    D. respect is based on the individual, and fear is based on the organization as a whole

17.____

18. If one of the employees you supervise does outstanding work, you should
    A. explain to him how his work can still be improved so that he will not become self-satisfied
    B. mildly criticize the other men for not doing as good a job as this man
    C. praise him for his work so that he will know it is appreciated
    D. say nothing or he might become conceited

18.____

19. A supervisor can BEST help establish good morale among his employees if he
    A. confides in them about his personal problems in order to encourage them to confide in him
    B. encourages them to become friendly with him but discourages social engagements with them
    C. points out to them the advantages of having a cooperative spirit in the department
    D. sticks to the same rules that he expects them to follow

19.____

20. The one of the following situations which would seem to indicate poor scheduling of work by the supervisor is
    A. everybody seeming to be very busy at the same time
    B. re-assignment of a man to other work because of breakdown of a piece of equipment
    C. two employees on vacation at the same time
    D. two operators waiting to use the same equipment at the same time

20.____

KEY (CORRECT ANSWERS)

1.	B	11.	C
2.	D	12.	D
3.	B	13.	A
4.	C	14.	B
5.	D	15.	C
6.	A	16.	B
7.	A	17.	C
8.	C	18.	C
9.	C	19.	D
10.	D	20.	D

EXAMINATION SECTION
TEST 1

DIRECTIONS: Each question or incomplete statement is followed by several suggested answers or completions. Select the one that BEST answers the question or completes the statement. *PRINT THE LETTER OF THE CORRECT ANSWER IN THE SPACE AT THE RIGHT.*

1. Which of the following is the MOST likely action a supervisor should take to help establish an effective working relationship with his departmental superiors?
    A. Delay the implementation of new procedures received from superiors in order to evaluate their appropriateness.
    B. Skip the chain of command whenever he feels that it is to his advantage
    C. Keep supervisors informed of problems in his area and the steps taken to correct them
    D. Don't take up superiors' time by discussing anticipated problems but wait until the difficulties occur

1.____

2. Of the following, the action a supervisor could take which would generally be MOST conducive to the establishment of an effective working relationship with employees includes
    A. maintaining impersonal relationships to prevent development of biased actions
    B. treating all employees equally without adjusting for individual differences
    C. continuous observation of employees on the job with insistence on constant improvement
    D. careful planning and scheduling of work for your employees

2.____

3. Which of the following procedures is the LEAST likely to establish effective working relationships between employees and supervisors?
    A. Encouraging two-way communication with employees
    B. Periodic discussion with employees regarding their job performance
    C. Ignoring employees' gripes concerning job difficulties
    D. Avoiding personal prejudices in dealing with employees

3.____

4. Criticism can be used as a tool to point out the weak areas of a subordinate's work performance.
Of the following, the BEST action for a supervisor to take so that his criticism will be accepted is to
    A. focus his criticism on the act instead of on the person
    B. exaggerate the errors in order to motivate the employee to do better
    C. pass judgment quickly and privately without investigating the circumstances of the error
    D. generalize the criticism and not specifically point out the errors in performance

4.____

5. In trying to improve the motivation of his subordinates, a supervisor can achieve the BEST results by taking action based upon the assumption that most employees
   A. have an inherent dislike of work
   B. wish to be closely directed
   C. are more interested in security than in assuming responsibility
   D. will exercise self-direction without coercion

6. When there are conflicts or tensions between top management and lower-level employees in any department, the supervisor should FIRST attempt to
   A. represent and enforce the management point of view
   B. act as the representative of the workers to get their ideas across to management
   C. serve as a two-way spokesman, trying to interpret each side to the other
   D. remain neutral, but keep informed of changes in the situation

7. A probationary period for new employees is usually provided in many agencies. The MAJOR purpose of such a period is usually to
   A. allow a determination of employee's suitability for the position
   B. obtain evidence as to employee's ability to perform in a higher position
   C. conform to requirements that ethnic hiring goals be met for all positions
   D. train the new employee in the duties of the position

8. An effective program of orientation for new employees usually includes all of the following EXCEPT
   A. having the supervisor introduce the new employee to his job, outlining his responsibilities and how to carry them out
   B. permitting the new worker to tour the facility or department so he can observe all parts of it in action
   C. scheduling meetings for new employees, at which the job requirements are explained to them and they are given personnel manuals
   D. testing the new worker on his skills and sending him to a centralized in-service workshop

9. In-service training is an important responsibility of many supervisors. The MAJOR reason for such training is to
   A. avoid future grievance procedures because employees might say they were not prepared to carry out their jobs
   B. maximize the effectiveness of the department by helping each employee perform at his full potential
   C. satisfy inspection teams from central headquarters of the department
   D. help prevent disagreements with members of the community

10. There are many forms of useful in-service training.
    Of the following, the training method which is NOT an appropriate technique for leadership development is to
    A. provide special workshops or clinics in activity skills
    B. conduct institutes to familiarize new workers with the program of the department and with their roles

C. schedule team meetings for problem-solving, including both supervisors and leaders
D. have the leader rate himself on an evaluation form periodically

11. Of the following techniques of evaluating work training programs, the one that is BEST is to
    A. pass out a carefully designed questionnaire to the trainees at the completion of the program
    B. test the knowledge that trainees have both at the beginning of training and at its completion
    C. interview the trainees at the completion of the program
    D. evaluate performance before and after training for both a control group and an experimental group

12. Assume that a new supervisor is having difficulty making his instructions to subordinates clearly understood.
    The one of the following which is the FIRST step he should take in dealing with this problem is to
    A. set up a training workshop in communication skills
    B. determine the extent and nature of the communications gap
    C. repeat both verbal and written instructions several times
    D. simplify his written and spoken vocabulary

13. A director has not properly carried out the orders of his assistant supervisor on several occasions to the point where he has been successively warned, reprimanded, and severely reprimanded.
    When the director once again does not carry out orders, the PROPER action for the assistant supervisor to take is to
    A. bring the director up on charges of failing to perform his duties properly
    B. have a serious discussion with the director, explaining the need for the orders and the necessity for carrying them out
    C. recommend that the director be transferred to another district
    D. severely reprimand the director again, making clear that no further deviation will be countenanced

14. A supervisor with several subordinates becomes aware that two of these subordinates are neither friendly nor congenial.
    In making assignments, it would be BEST for the supervisor to
    A. disregard the situation
    B. disregard the situation in making a choice of assignment but emphasize the need for teamwork
    C. investigate the situation to find out who is at fault and give that individual the less desirable assignments until such time as he corrects his attitude
    D. place the unfriendly subordinates in positions where they have as little contact with one another as possible

15. A DESIRABLE characteristic of a good supervisor is that he should
    A. identify himself with his subordinates rather than with higher management
    B. inform subordinates of forthcoming changes in policies and programs only when they directly affect the subordinates' activities
    C. make advancement of the subordinates contingent on personal loyalty to the supervisor
    D. make promises to subordinates only when sure of the ability to keep them

16. The supervisor who is MOST likely to be successful is the one who
    A. refrains from exercising the special privileges of his position
    B. maintains a formal attitude toward his subordinates
    C. maintains an informal attitude toward his subordinates
    D. represents the desires of his subordinate to his superiors

17. Application of sound principles of human relations by a supervisor may be expected to _____ the need for formal discipline.
    A. decrease   B. have no effect on
    C. increase   D. obviate

18. The MOST important generally approved way to maintain or develop high morale in one's subordinates is to
    A. give warnings and reprimands in a jocular way
    B. excuse from staff conferences those employees who are busy
    C. keep them informed of new developments and policies of higher management
    D. refrain from criticizing their faults directly

19. In training subordinates, an IMPORTANT principle for the supervisor to recognize is that
    A. a particular method of instruction will be of substantially equal value for all employees in a given title
    B. it is difficult to train people over 50 years of age because they have little capacity for learning
    C. persons undergoing the same course of training will learn at different rates of speed
    D. training can seldom achieve its purpose unless individual instruction is the chief method used

20. Over an extended period of time, a subordinate is MOST likely to become and remain most productive if the supervisor
    A. accords praise to the subordinate whenever his work is satisfactory, withholding criticism except in the case of very inferior work
    B. avoids both praise and criticism except for outstandingly good or bad work performed by the subordinate
    C. informs the subordinate of his shortcomings, as viewed by management, while according praise only when highly deserved
    D. keeps the subordinate informed of the degree of satisfaction with which his performance of the job is viewed by management.

KEY (CORRECT ANSWERS)

1.	C	11.	D
2.	D	12.	B
3.	C	13.	A
4.	A	14.	D
5.	D	15.	D
6.	C	16.	D
7.	A	17.	A
8.	D	18.	C
9.	B	19.	C
10.	D	20.	D

TEST 2

DIRECTIONS: Each question or incomplete statement is followed by several suggested answers or completions. Select the one that BEST answers the question or completes the statement. *PRINT THE LETTER OF THE CORRECT ANSWER IN THE SPACE AT THE RIGHT.*

1. A supervisor has just been told by a subordinate, Mr. Jones, that another employee, Mr. Smith, deliberately disobeyed an important rule of the department by taking home some confidential departmental material.
   Of the following courses of action, it would be MOST advisable for the supervisor FIRST to
   A. discuss the matter privately with both Mr. Jones and Mrs. Smith at the same time
   B. call a meeting of the entire staff and discuss the matter generally without mentioning any employee by name
   C. arrange to supervise Mr. Smith's activities more closely
   D. discuss the matter privately with Mr. Smith

   1.____

2. The one of the following actions which would be MOST efficient and economical for a supervisor to take to minimize the effect of periodical fluctuations in the workload of his unit is to
   A. increase his permanent staff until it is large enough to handle the work of the busy loads
   B. request the purchase of time- and labor-saving equipment to be used primarily during the busy loads
   C. lower, temporarily, the standards for quality of work performance during peak loads
   D. schedule for the slow periods work that is not essential to perform during the busy periods

   2.____

3. Discipline of employees is usually a supervisor's responsibility. There may be several useful forms of disciplinary action.
   Of the following, the form that is LEAST appropriate is the
   A. written reprimand or warning
   B. involuntary transfer to another work setting
   C. demotion or suspension
   D. assignment of added hours of work each week

   3.____

4. Of the following, the MOST effective means of dealing with employee disciplinary problems is to
   A. give personality tests to individuals to identify their psychological problems
   B. distribute and discuss a policy manual containing exact rules governing employee behavior
   C. establish a single, clear penalty to be imposed for all wrongdoing irrespective of degree
   D. have supervisors get to know employees well through social mingling

   4.____

2 (#2)

5. A recently developed technique for appraising work performance is to have the supervisor record on a continual basis all significant incidents in each subordinate's behavior that indicate unsuccessful action and those that indicate poor behavior.
Of the following, a MAJOR disadvantage of this method of performance appraisal is that it
   A. often leads to overly close supervision
   B. results in competition among those subordinates being evaluated
   C. tends to result in superficial judgments
   D. lacks objectivity for evaluating performance

5.____

6. Assume that you are a supervisor and have observed the performance of an employee during a period of time. You have concluded that his performance needs improvement.
In order to improve his performance, it would, therefore, be BEST for you to
   A. note your findings in the employee's personnel folder so that his behavior is a matter of record
   B. report the findings to the personnel officer so he can take prompt action
   C. schedule a problem-solving conference with the employee
   D. recommend his transfer to simpler duties

6.____

7. When an employee's absences or latenesses seem to be nearing excessiveness, the supervisor should speak with him to find out what the problem is.
Of the following, if such a discussion produces no reasonable explanation, the discussion usually BEST serves to
   A. affirm clearly the supervisor's adherence to proper policy
   B. alert other employees that such behavior is unacceptable
   C. demonstrate that the supervisor truly represents higher management
   D. notify the employee that his behavior is being observed and evaluated

7.____

8. Assume that an employee willfully and recklessly violates an important agency regulation. The nature of the violation is of such magnitude that it demands immediate action, but the facts of the case are not entirely clear. Further, assume that the supervisor is free to make any of the following recommendations.
The MOST appropriate action for the supervisor to take is to recommend that the employee be
   A. discharged   B. suspended
   C. forced to resign   D. transferred

8.____

9. Although employees' titles may be identical, each position in that title may be considerably different.
Of the following, a supervisor should carefully assign each employee to a specific position based PRIMARILY on the employee's
   A. capability   B. experience   C. education   D. seniority

9.____

10. The one of the following situations where it is MOST appropriate to transfer an employee to a similar assignment is one in which the employee
    A. lacks motivation and interest
    B. experiences a personality conflict with his supervisor
    C. is negligent in the performance of his duties
    D. lacks capacity or ability to perform assigned tasks

11. The one of the following which is LEAST likely to be affected by improvements in the morale of personnel is employee
    A. skill
    B. absenteeism
    C. turnover
    D. job satisfaction

12. The one of the following situations in which it is LEAST appropriate for a supervisor to delegate authority to subordinates is where the supervisor
    A. lacks confidence in his own abilities to perform certain work
    B. is overburdened and cannot handle all his responsibilities
    C. refers all disciplinary problems to his subordinate
    D. has to deal with an emergency or crisis

13. Assume that it has come to your attention that two of your subordinates have shouted at each other and have almost engaged in a fist fight. Luckily, they were separated by some of the other employees.
    Of the following, your BEST immediate course of action would generally be to
    A. reprimand the senior of the two subordinates since he should have known better
    B. hear the story from both employees and any witnesses and then take needed disciplinary action
    C. ignore the matter since nobody was physically hurt
    D. immediately suspend and fine both employees pending a departmental hearing

14. You have been delegating some of your authority to one of your subordinates because of his leadership potential.
    Which of the following actions is LEAST conducive to the growth and development of this individual for a supervisory position?
    A. Use praise only when it will be effective
    B. Give very detailed instructions and supervise the employee closely to be sure that the instructions ae followed precisely
    C. Let the subordinate proceed with his planned course of action even if mistakes, within a permissible range, are made
    D. Intervene on behalf of the subordinate whenever an assignment becomes difficult for him

15. A rumor has been spreading in your department concerning the possibility of layoffs due to decreased revenues.
    As a supervisor, you should GENERALLY
    A. deny the rumor, whether it is true or false, in order to keep morale from declining

B. inform the men to the best of your knowledge about this situation and keep them advised of any new information
C. tell the men to forget about the rumor and concentrate on increasing their productivity
D. ignore the rumor since it is not authorized information

16. Within an organization, every supervisor should know to whom he reports and who reports to him.
The one of the following which is achieved by use of such structured relationships is
    A. unity of command
    B. confidentiality
    C. esprit de corps
    D. promotion opportunities

16._____

17. Almost every afternoon, one of your employees comes back from his break ten minutes late without giving you any explanation.
Which of the following actions should you take FIRST in this situation?
    A. Assign the employee to a different type of work and observe whether his behavior changes
    B. Give the employee extra work to do so that he will have to return on time
    C. Ask the employee for an explanation for his lateness
    D. Tell the employee he is jeopardizing the break for everyone

17._____

18. When giving instructions to your employees in a group, which one of the following should you make certain to do?
    A. Speak in a casual, off-hand manner
    B. Assume that your employees fully understand the instructions
    C. Write out your instructions beforehand and read them to the employees
    D. Tell exactly who is to do what

18._____

19. A fist fight develops between two men under your supervision.
The MOST advisable course of action for you to take FIRST is to
    A. call the police
    B. have the other workers pull them apart
    C. order them to stop
    D. step between the two men

19._____

20. You have assigned some difficult and unusual work to one of your most experienced and competent subordinates.
If you notice that he is doing the work incorrectly, you should
    A. assign the work to another employee
    B. reprimand him in private
    C. show him immediately how the work should be done
    D. wait until the job is completed and then correct his errors

20._____

KEY (CORRECT ANSWERS)

1.	D	11.	A
2.	D	12.	C
3.	D	13.	B
4.	B	14.	B
5.	A	15.	B
6.	C	16.	A
7.	D	17.	C
8.	B	18.	D
9.	A	19.	C
10.	B	20.	C

PREPARING WRITTEN MATERIAL

PARAGRAPH REARRANGEMENT
COMMENTARY

The sentences that follow are in scrambled order. You are to rearrange them in proper order and indicate the letter choice containing the correct answer at the space at the right.

Each group of sentences in this section is actually a paragraph presented in scrambled order. Each sentence in the group has a place in that paragraph; no sentence is to be left out. You are to read each group of sentences and decide upon the best order in which to put the sentences so as to form a well-organized paragraph.

The questions in this section measure the ability to solve a problem when all the facts relevant to its solution are not given.

More specifically, certain positions of responsibility and authority require the employee to discover connection between events sometimes, apparently, unrelated. In order to do this, the employee will find it necessary to correctly infer that unspecified events have probably occurred or are likely to occur. This ability becomes especially important when action must be taken on incomplete information.

Accordingly, these questions require competitors to choose among several suggested alternatives, each of which presents a different sequential arrangement of the events. Competitors must choose the MOST logical of the suggested sequences.

In order to do so, they may be required to draw on general knowledge to infer missing concepts or events that are essential to sequencing the given events. Competitors should be careful to infer only what is essential to the sequence. The plausibility of the wrong alternatives will always require the inclusion of unlikely events or of additional chains of events which are NOT essential to sequencing the given events.

It's very important to remember that you are looking for the best of the four possible choices, and that the best choice of all may not even be one of the answers you're given to choose from.

There is no one right way to solve these problems. Many people have found it helpful to first write out the order of the sentences, as they would have arranged them, on their scrap paper before looking at the possible answers. If their optimum answer is there, this can save them some time. If it isn't, this method can still give insight into solving the problem. Others find it most helpful to just go through each of the possible choices, contrasting each as they go along. You should use whatever method feels comfortable and works for you.

While most of these types of questions are not that difficult, we've added a higher percentage of the difficult type, just to give you more practice. Usually there are only one or two questions on this section that contain such subtle distinctions that you're unable to answer confidently. And you then may find yourself stuck deciding between two possible choices, neither of which you're sure about.

EXAMINATION SECTION

TEST 1

DIRECTIONS: The sentences that follow are in scrambled order. You are to rearrange them in proper order and indicate the letter choice containing the correct answer. *PRINT THE LETTER OF THE CORRECT ANSWER IN THE SPACE AT THE RIGHT.*

1. Below are four statements labeled W, X, Y and Z. 1.____
   W. He was a strict and fanatic drillmaster.
   X. The word is always used in a derogatory sense and generally shows resentment and anger on the part of the user.
   Y. It is from the name of this Frenchman that we derive our English word, martinet.
   Z. Jean Martinet was the Inspector-General of Infantry during the reign of King Louis XIV.
   The PROPER order in which these sentences should be placed in a paragraph is:
   A. X, Z, W, Y   B. X, Z, Y, W   C. Z, W, Y, X   D. Z, Y, W, X

2. In the following paragraph, the sentences, which are numbered, have been jumbled. 2.____
   I. Since then it has undergone changes.
   II. It was incorporated in 1955 under the laws of the State of New York.
   III. Its primary purposes, a cleaner city, has, however, remained the same.
   IV. The Citizens Committee works in cooperation with the Mayor's Inter-
       departmental Committee for a Clean City. 3.____
   The order in which these sentences should be arranged to form a well-organized paragraph is:
   A. II, IV, I, III   B. III, IV, I, II   C. IV, II, I, III   D. IV, III, II, I

Questions 3-5.

DIRECTIONS: The sentences listed below are part of a meaningful paragraph but they are not given in their proper order. You are to decide what would be the BEST order in which to put the sentences so as to form a well-organized paragraph. Each sentence has a place in the paragraph; there are no extra sentences. You are then to answer Questions 3 through 5 inclusive on the basis of your rearrangements of these scrambled sentences into a properly organized paragraph.

In 1887 some insurance companies organized an Inspection Department to advise their clients on all phases of fire prevention and protection. Probably this has been due to the smaller annual fire losses in Great Britain than in the United States. It tests various fire prevention devices and appliances and determines manufacturing hazards and their safeguards. Fire research began earlier in the United States and is more advanced than in Great Britain. Later they established a laboratory specializing in electrical, mechanical, hydraulic, and chemical fields.

3. When the five sentences are arranged in proper order, the paragraph starts with the sentence which begins
   A. "In 1887..."   B. "Probably this..."   C. "It tests..."
   D. "Fire research..."   E. "Later they..."

3._____

4. In the last sentence listed above, "they" refers to
   A. the insurance companies
   B. the United States and Great Britain
   C. the Inspection Department
   D. clients
   E. technicians

4._____

5. When the above paragraph is properly arranged, it ends with the words
   A. "...and protection."   B. "...the United States."
   C. "...their safeguards."   D. "...in Great Britain."
   E. "...chemical fields."

5._____

KEY (CORRECT ANSWERS)

1. C
2. C
3. D
4. A
5. C

TEST 2

DIRECTIONS: In each of the questions numbered I through V, several sentences are given. For each question, choose as your answer the group of number that represents the MOST logical order of these sentences if they were arranged in paragraph form. *PRINT THE LETTER OF THE CORRECT ANSWER IN THE SPACE AT THE RIGHT.*

1.
   I. It is established when one shows that the landlord has prevented the tenant's enjoyment of his interest in the property leased.
   II. Constructive eviction is the result of a breach of the covenant of quiet enjoyment implied in all leases.
   III. In some parts of the United States, it is not complete until the tenant vacates within a reasonable time.
   IV. Generally, the acts must be of such serious and permanent character as to deny the tenant the enjoyment of his possessing rights.
   V. In this event, upon abandonment of the premises, the tenant's liability for that ceases.
   The CORRECT answer is:
   A. II, I, IV, III, V
   B. V, II, III, I, IV
   C. IV, III, I, II, V
   D. I, III, V, IV, II

2.
   I. The powerlessness before private and public authorities that is the typical experience of the slum tenant is reminiscent of the situation of blue-collar workers all through the nineteenth century.
   II. Similarly, in recent years, this chapter of history has been reopened by anti-poverty groups which have attempted to organize slum tenants to enable them to bargain collectively with their landlords about the conditions of their tenancies.
   III. It is familiar history that many of the worker remedied their condition by joining together and presenting their demands collectively.
   IV. Like the workers, tenants are forced by the conditions of modern life into substantial dependence on these who possess great political aid and economic power.
   V. What's more, the very fact of dependence coupled with an absence of education and self-confidence makes them hesitant and unable to stand up for what they need from those in power.
   The CORRECT answer is:
   A. V, IV, I, II, III
   B. II, III, I, V, IV
   C. III, I, V, IV, II
   D. I, IV, V, III, II

3.
   I. A railroad, for example, when not acting as a common carrier may contract away responsibility for its own negligence.
   II. As to a landlord, however, no decision has been found relating to the legal effect of a clause shifting the statutory duty of repair to the tenant.
   III. The courts have not passed on the validity of clauses relieving the landlord of this duty and liability.
   IV. They have, however, upheld the validity of exculpatory clauses in other types of contracts.

V. Housing regulations impose a duty upon the landlord to maintain leased premises in safe condition.
VI. As another example, a bailee may limit his liability except for gross negligence, willful acts, or fraud.

The CORRECT answer is:
- A. II, I, VI, IV, III, V
- B. I, III, IV, V, VI, II
- C. III, V, I, IV, II, VI
- D. V, III, IV, I, VI, II

4.
I. Since there are only samples in the building, retail or consumer sales are generally eschewed by mart occupants, and in some instances, rigid controls are maintained to limit entrance to the mart only to those persons engaged in retailing.
II. Since World War I, in many larger cities, there has developed a new type of property, called the mart building.
III. It can, therefore, be used by wholesalers and jobbers for the display of sample merchandise.
IV. This type of building is most frequently a multi-storied, finished interior property which is a cross between a retail arcade and a loft building.
V. This limitation enables the mart occupants to ship the orders from another location after the retailer or dealer makes his selection from the samples.

The CORRECT answer is:
- A. II, IV, III, I, V
- B. IV, III, V, I, II
- C. I, III, II, IV, V
- D. I, IV, II, III, V

4.____

5.
I. In general, staff-line friction reduces the distinctive contribution of staff personnel.
II. The conflicts, however, introduce an uncontrolled element into the managerial system.
III. On the other hand, the natural resistance of the line to staff innovations probably usefully restrains over-eager efforts to apply untested procedures on a large scale.
IV. Under such conditions, it is difficult to know when valuable ideas are being sacrificed.
V. The relatively weak position of staff, requiring accommodation to the line, tends to restrict their ability to engage in free, experimental innovation.

The CORRECT answer is:
- A. IV, II, III, I, V
- B. I, V, III, II, IV
- C. V, III, I, II, IV
- D. II, I, IV, V, III

5.____

KEY (CORRECT ANSWERS)

1. A
2. D
3. D
4. A
5. B

TEST 3

DIRECTIONS: Questions 1 through 4 consist of six sentences which can be arranged in a logical sequence. For each question, select the choice which places the numbered sentences in the MOST logical sequent. *PRINT THE LETTER OF THE CORRECT ANSWER IN THE SPACE AT THE RIGHT.*

1.
   I. The burden of proof as to each issue is determined before trial and remains upon the same party throughout the trial.
   II. The jury is at liberty to believe one witness' testimony as against a number of contradictory witnesses.
   III. In a civil case, the party bearing the burden of proof is required to prove his contention by a fair preponderance of the evidence.
   IV. However, it must be noted that a fair preponderance of evidence does not necessarily mean a greater number of witnesses.
   V. The burden of proof is the burden which rests upon one of the parties to an action to persuade the trier of the facts, generally the jury, that a proposition he asserts is true.
   VI. If the evidence is equally balanced, or if it leaves the jury in such doubt as to be unable to decide the controversy either way, judgment must be given against the party upon whom the burden of proof rests.
   The CORRECT answer is:
   A. III, II, V, IV, I, VI
   B. I, II, VI, V, III, IV
   C. III, IV, V, I, II, VI
   D. V, I, III, VI, IV, II

   1.____

2.
   I. If a parent is without assets and is unemployed, he cannot be convicted of the crime of non-support of a child.
   II. The term "sufficient ability" has been held to mean sufficient financial ability.
   III. It does not matter if his unemployment is by choice or unavoidable circumstances.
   IV. If he fails to take any steps at all, he may be liable to prosecution for endangering the welfare of a child.
   V. Under the penal law, a parent is responsible for the support of his minor child only if the parent is "of sufficient ability."
   VI. An indigent parent may meet his obligation by borrowing money or by seeking aid under the provisions of the Social Welfare Law.
   The CORRECT answer is:
   A. VI, I, V, III, II, IV
   B. I, III, V, II, IV, VI
   C. V, II, I, III, VI, IV
   D. I, VI, IV, V, II, III

   2.____

3.
   I. Consider, for example, the case of a rabble rouser who urges a group of twenty people to go out and break the windows of a nearby factory.
   II. Therefore, the law fills the indicated gap with the crime of inciting to riot.
   III. A person is considered guilty of inciting to riot when he urges ten or more persons to engage in tumultuous and violent conduct of a kind likely to create public alarm.
   IV. However, if he has not obtained the cooperation of at least four people, he cannot be charged with unlawful assembly.

   3.____

V. The charge of inciting to riot was added to the law to cover types of conduct which cannot be classified as either the crime of "riot" or the crime of "unlawful assembly."
VI. If he acquires the acquiescence of at least four of them, he is guilty of unlawful assembly even if the project does not materialize.

The CORRECT answer is:
- A. III, V, I, VI, IV, II
- B. V, I, IV, VI, II, III
- C. III, IV, I, V, II, VI
- D. V, I, IV, VI, III, II

4.
I. If, however, the rebuttal evidence presents an issue of credibility, it is for the jury to determine whether the presumption has, in fact, been destroyed.
II. Once sufficient evidence to the contrary is introduced, the presumption disappears from the trial.
III. The effect of a presumption is to place the burden upon the adversary to come forward with evidence to rebut the presumption.
IV. When a presumption is overcome and ceases to exist in the case, the fact or facts which gave rise to the presumption still remain.
V. Whether a presumption has been overcome is ordinarily a question for the court.
VI. Such information may furnish a basis for a logical inference.

The CORRECT answer is:
- A. IV, VI, II, V, I, III
- B. III, II, V, I, IV, VI
- C. V, III, VI, IV, II, I
- D. V, IV, I, II, VI, III

KEY (CORRECT ANSWERS)

1. D
2. C
3. A
4. B

PREPARING WRITTEN MATERIALS
EXAMINATION SECTION
TEST 1

DIRECTIONS: Each question or incomplete statement is followed by several suggested answers or completions. Select the one that BEST answers the question or completes the statement. *PRINT THE LETTER OF THE CORRECT ANSWER IN THE SPACE AT THE RIGHT.*

Questions 1-25.

DIRECTIONS: Questions 1 through 25 consist of sentences which may or may not be examples of good English usage. Consider grammar, punctuation, spelling, capitalization, awkwardness, etc. Examine each sentence and then choose the correct statement about it from the four choices below it. If the English usage in the sentence given is better than it would be with any of the changes suggested in options B, C, and D, choose option A. Do not choose an option that will change the meaning of the sentence.

1. According to Judge Frank, the grocer's sons found guilty of assault and sentenced last Thursday.
   A. This is an example of acceptable writing.
   B. A comma should be placed after the word *sentenced*.
   C. The word *were* should be placed after *sons*.
   D. The apostrophe in grocer's should be placed after the *s*.

2. The department heads assistant said that the stenographers should type duplicate copies of all contracts, leases, and bills.
   A. This is an example of acceptable writing,
   B. A comma should be placed before the word "*contracts*.
   C. An apostrophe should be placed before the *s* in *heads*.
   D. Quotation marks should be placed before the *stenographers* and after *bills*.

3. The lawyers questioned the men to determine who was the true property owner?
   A. This is an example of acceptable writing.
   B. The phrase *questioned the men* should be changed to *asked the men questions*.
   C. The word *was* should be changed to *were*.
   D. The question mark should be changed to a period.

4. The terms stated in the present contract are more specific than those stated in the previous contract.
   A. This is an example of acceptable writing,
   B. The word *are* should be changed to *is*.
   C. The word *than* should be changed to *then*.
   D. The word *specific* should be changed to *specified*.

   4._____

5. Of the few lawyers considered, the one who argued more skillful was chosen for the job.
   A. This is an example of acceptable writing.
   B. The word *more* should be replaced by the word *most*.
   C. The word *skillful* should be replaced by the word *skillfully*.
   D. The word *chosen* should be replaced by the word *selected*.

   5._____

6. Each of the states has a court of appeals; some states have circuit courts.
   A. This is an example of acceptable writing
   B. The semi-colon should be changed to a comma.
   C. The word *has* should be changed to *have*.
   D. The word *some* should be capitalized.

   6._____

7. The court trial has greatly effected the child's mental condition.
   A. This is an example of acceptable writing.
   B. The word *effected* should be changed to *affected*.
   C. The word *greatly* should be placed after *effected*.
   D. The apostrophe in *child's* should be placed after the *s*.

   7._____

8. Last week, the petition signed by all the officers was sent to the Better Business Bureau.
   A. This is an example of acceptable writing.
   B. The phrase *last week* should be placed after *officers*.
   C. A comma should be placed after *petition*.
   D. The word *was* should be changed to *were*.

   8._____

9. Mr. Farrell claims that he requested form A-12, and three booklets describing court procedures.
   A. This is an example of acceptable writing.
   B. The word *that* should be eliminated.
   C. A colon should be placed after *requested*.
   D. The comma after *A-12* should be eliminated.

   9._____

10. We attended a staff conference on Wednesday the new safety and fire rules were discussed.
    A. This is an example of acceptable writing.
    B. The words *safety*, *fire*, and *rules* should begin with capital letters.
    C. There should be a comma after the word *Wednesday*.
    D. There should be a period after the word *Wednesday*, and the word *the* should begin with a capital letter.

    10._____

11. Neither the dictionary or the telephone directory could be found in the office library.   11.____
    A. This is an example of acceptable writing.
    B. The word *or* should be changed to *nor*.
    C. The word *library* should be spelled *libery*.
    D. The word *neither* should be changed to *either*.

12. The report would have been typed correctly if the typist could read the draft.   12.____
    A. This is an example of acceptable writing.
    B. The word *would* should be removed.
    C. The word *have* should be inserted after the word *could*.
    D. The word *correctly* should be changed to *correct*.

13. The supervisor brought the reports and forms to an employees desk.   13.____
    A. This is an example of acceptable writing.
    B. The word *brought* should be changed to *took*.
    C. There should be a comma after the word *reports* and a comma after the word *forms*.
    D. The word *employees* should be spelled *employee's*.

14. It's important for all the office personnel to submit their vacation schedules on time.   14.____
    A. This is an example of acceptable writing.
    B. The word *It's* should be spelled *Its*.
    C. The word *their* should be spelled *they're*.
    D. The word *personnel* should be spelled *personal*.

15. The supervisor wants that all staff members report to the office at 9:00 A.M.   15.____
    A. This is an example of acceptable writing.
    B. The word *that* should be removed and the word *to* should be inserted after the word *members*.
    C. There should be a comma after the word *wants* and a comma after the word *office*.
    D. The word *wants* should be changed to *want* and the word *shall* should be inserted after the word *members*.

16. Every morning the clerk opens the office mail and distributes it.   16.____
    A. This is an example of acceptable writing.
    B. The word *opens* should be changed to *letters*.
    C. The word *mail* should be changed to *letters*.
    D. The word *it* should be changed to *them*.

17. The secretary typed more fast on a desktop computer than on a tablet.   17.____
    A. This is an example of acceptable writing.
    B. The words *more fast* should be changed to *faster*.
    C. There should be a comma after the words *desktop computer*.
    D. The word *than* should be changed to *then*.

18. The typist used an extention cord in order to connect her typewriter to the outlet nearest to her desks.
    A. This is an example of acceptable writing.
    B. A period should be placed after the word *cord*, and the word *in* should have a capital *I*.
    C. A comma should be placed after the word *typewriter*.
    D. The word *extention* should be spelled *extension*.

19. He would have went to the conference if he had received an invitation.
    A. This is an example of acceptable writing.
    B. The word *went* should be replaced by the word *gone*.
    C. The word *had* should be replaced by *would have*.
    D. The word *conference* should be spelled *conferance*.

20. In order to make the report neater, he spent many hours rewriting it.
    A. This is an example of acceptable writing.
    B. The word *more* should be inserted before the word *neater*.
    C. There should be a colon after the word *neater*.
    D. The word *spent* should be changed to *have spent*.

21. His supervisor told him that he should of read the memorandum more carefully.
    A. This is an example of acceptable writing.
    B. The word *memorandum* should be spelled *memorandom*.
    C. The word *of* should be replaced by the word *have*.
    D. The word *carefully* should be replaced by the word *careful*.

22. It was decided that two separate reports should be written.
    A. This is an example of acceptable writing.
    B. A comma should be inserted after the word *decided*.
    C. The word *be* should be replaced by the word *been*.
    D. A colon should be inserted after the word *that*.

23. She don't seem to understand that the work must be done as soon as possible.
    A. This is an example of acceptable writing.
    B. The word *doesn't* should replace the word *don't*.
    C. The word *why* should replace the word *that*.
    D. The word *as* before the word *soon* should be eliminated.

24. He excepted praise from his supervisor for a job well done.
    A. This is an example of acceptable writing.
    B. The word *excepted* should be spelled *accepted*.
    C. The order of the words *well done* should be changed to *done well*.
    D. There should be a comma after the word *supervisor*.

25. What appears to be intentional errors in grammar occur several times in the passage.
    A. This is an example of acceptable writing.
    B. The word *occur* should be spelled *occur*.
    C. The word *appears* should be changed to *appear*.
    D. The phrase *several times* should be changed to *from time to time*.

25.____

KEY (CORRECT ANSWERS)

1.	C	11.	B
2.	C	12.	C
3.	D	13.	D
4.	A	14.	A
5.	C	15.	B
6.	A	16.	A
7.	B	17.	B
8.	A	18.	D
9.	D	19.	B
10.	D	20.	A

21. C
22. A
23. B
24. B
25. C

TEST 2

DIRECTIONS: Each question consists of a sentence which may or may not be an example of good formal English usage. Examine each sentence, considering grammar, punctuation, spelling, capitalization, and awkwardness. Then choose the CORRECT statement about it from the four options below it. If the English usage in the sentence given is better than any of the changes suggested in options B, C, or D, pick option A. Do not pick an option that will change the meaning of the sentence. *PRINT THE LETTER OF THE CORRECT ANSWER IN THE SPACE AT THE RIGHT.*

1. I don't know who could possibly of broken it.
   A. This is an example of acceptable writing.
   B. The word *who* should be replaced by the word *whom*.
   C. The word *of* should be replaced by the word *have*.
   D. The word *broken* should be replaced by the word *broke*.

2. Telephoning is easier than to write.
   A. This is an example of acceptable writing.
   B. The word *telephoning* should be spelled *telephoneing*.
   C. The word *than* should be replaced by the word *then*.
   D. The words *to write* should be replaced by the word *writing*.

3. The two operators who have been assigned to these consoles are on vacation.
   A. This is an example of acceptable writing.
   B. A comma should be placed after the word *operators*.
   C. The word *who* should be replaced by the word *whom*.
   D. The word *are* should be replaced by the word *is*.

4. You were suppose to teach me how to operate a plugboard.
   A. This is an example of acceptable writing,
   B. The word *were* should be replaced by the word *was*.
   C. The word *suppose* should be replaced by the word *supposed*.
   D. The word *teach* should be replaced by the word *team*.

5. If you had taken my advice; you would have spoken with him.
   A. This is an example of acceptable writing.
   B. The word *advice* should be spelled *advise*.
   C. The words *had taken* should be replaced by the word *take*.
   D. The semicolon should be changed to a comma.

6. The clerk could have completed the assignment on time if he knows where these materials were located.
   A. This is an example of acceptable writing.
   B. The word *knows* should be replaced by *had known*.
   C. The word "were" should be replaced by *had been*.
   D. The words *where these materials were located* should be replaced by *the location of these materials*.

7. All employees should be given safety training. Not just those who have accidents.
    A. This is an example of acceptable writing,
    B. The period after the word *training* should be changed to a colon.
    C. The period after the word *training* should be changed to a semicolon, and the first letter of the word *Not* should be changed to a small *n*.
    D. The period after the word *training* should be changed to a comma, and the first letter of the word *Not* should be changed to a small *n*,

8. This proposal is designed to promote employee awareness of the suggestion program, to encourage employee participation in the program, and to increase the number of suggestions submitted.
    A. This is an example of acceptable writing.
    B. The word *proposal* should be spelled *proposal*.
    C. The words *to increase the number of suggestions submitted* should be changed to *an increase in the number of suggestions is expected*.
    D. The word *promote* should be changed to *enhance*, and the word *increase* should be changed to *add to*.

9. The introduction of inovative managerial techniques should be preceded by careful analysis of the specific circumstances and conditions in each department.
    A. This is an example of acceptable writing.
    B. The word *techniques* should be spelled *techneques*.
    C. The word *inovative* should be spelled *innovative*.
    D. A comma should be placed after the word *circumstances* and after the word *conditions*.

10. This occurrence indicates that such criticism embarrasses him.
    A. This is an example of acceptable writing.
    B. The word *occurrence* should be spelled *occurence*.
    C. The word *criticism* should be spelled *creticism*.
    D. The word *embarrasses* should be spelled *embarasses*.

11. He can recommend a mechanic whose work is reliable.
    A. This is an example of acceptable writing.
    B. the word *reliable* should be spelled *relyable*.
    C. The word *whose* should be spelled *who's*.
    D. The word *mechanic* should be spelled *mecanic*.

12. She typed quickly; like someone who had not a moment to lose.
    A. This is an example of acceptable writing.
    B. The word *not* should be removed.
    C. The semicolon should be changed to a comma.
    D. The word *quickly* should be placed before instead of after the word *typed*.

13. She insisted that she had to much work to do. 13.____
    A. This is an example of acceptable writing.
    B. The word *insisted* should be spelled *insisted*.
    C. The word *to* used in front of *much* should be spelled *too*.
    D. The word *do* should be changed to *be done*.

14. The report, along with the accompanying documents, were submitted for review. 14.____
    A. This is an example of acceptable writing.
    B. The words *were submitted* should be changed to *was submitted*.
    C. The word *accompanying* should be spelled *accompaning*.
    D. The comma after the word *report* should be taken out.

15. If others must use your files, be certain that they understand how the system works, but insist that you do all the filing and refiling. 15.____
    A. This is an example of acceptable writing.
    B. There should be a period after the word *works*, and the word *but* should start a new sentence.
    C. The words *filing* and *refiling* should be spelled *fileing* and *refileing*.
    D. There should be a comma after the word *but*.

16. The appeal was not considered because of its late arrival. 16.____
    A. This is an example of acceptable writing.
    B. The word *its* should be changed to *it's*.
    C. The word *its* should be changed to *the*.
    D. The words *late arrival* should be changed to *arrival late*.

17. The letter must be read carefully to determine under which subject it should be filed. 17.____
    A. This is an example of acceptable writing.
    B. The word *under* should be changed to *at*.
    C. The word *determine* should be spelled *determin*.
    D. The word *carefully* should be spelled *carefully*.

18. He showed potential as an office manager, but he lacked skill in delegating work. 18.____
    A. This is an example of acceptable writing.
    B. The word *delegating* should be spelled *delagating*.
    C. The word *potential* should be spelled *potencial*.
    D. The words *he lacked* should be changed to *was lacking*.

19. His supervisor told him that it would be all right to receive personal mail at the office. 19.____
    A. This is an example of acceptable writing.
    B. The words *all right* should be changed to *alright*.
    C. The word *personal* should be spelled *personel*.
    D. The word *mail* should be changed to *letters*.

20. The report, along with the accompanying documents, were submitted for review. 20.____
    A. This is an example of acceptable writing.
    B. The words *were submitted* should be changed to *was submitted*.
    C. The word *accompanying* should be spelled *accompaning*.
    D. The comma after the word *report* should be taken out.

KEY (CORRECT ANSWERS)

1.	C	11.	A
2.	D	12.	C
3.	A	13.	C
4.	C	14.	B
5.	D	15.	A
6.	B	16.	A
7.	D	17.	D
8.	A	18.	A
9.	C	19.	A
10.	A	20.	B

PHILOSOPHY, PRINCIPLES, PRACTICES, AND TECHNICS
OF
SUPERVISION, ADMINISTRATION, MANAGEMENT, AND ORGANIZATION

TABLE OF CONTENTS

	Page
MEANING OF SUPERVISION	1
THE OLD AND THE NEW SUPERVISION	1
THE EIGHT (8) BASIC PRINCIPLES OF THE NEW SUPERVISION	1
I. Principle of Responsibility	1
II. Principle of Authority	2
III. Principle of Self-Growth	2
IV. Principle of Individual Worth	2
V. Principle of Creative Leadership	2
VI. Principle of Success and Failure	2
VII. Principle of Science	3
VIII. Principle of Cooperation	3
WHAT IS ADMINISTRATION?	3
I. Practices Commonly Classed as "Supervisory"	3
II. Practices Commonly Classed as "Administrative"	3
III. Practices Commonly Classed as Both "Supervisory" and "Administrative"	4
RESPONSIBILITIES OF THE SUPERVISOR	4
COMPETENCIES OF THE SUPERVISOR	4
THE PROFESSIONAL SUPERVISOR-EMPLOYEE RELATIONSHIP	4
MINI-TEXT IN SUPERVISION, ADMINISTRATION, MANAGEMENT, AND ORGANIZATION	5
I. Brief Highlights	5
A. Levels of Management	6
B. What the Supervisor Must Learn	6
C. A Definition of Supervision	6
D. Elements of the Team Concept	6
E. Principles of Organization	6
F. The Four Important Parts of Every Job	7
G. Principles of Delegation	7
H. Principles of Effective Communications	7
I. Principles of Work Improvement	7
J. Areas of Job Improvement	7
K. Seven Key Points in Making Improvements	8

L.	Corrective Techniques for Job Improvement		8
M.	A Planning Checklist		8
N.	Five Characteristics of Good Directions		9
O.	Types of Directions		9
P.	Controls		9
Q.	Orienting the New Employee		9
R.	Checklist for Orienting New Employees		9
S.	Principles of Learning		10
T.	Causes of Poor Performance		10
U.	Four Major Steps in On-the-Job Instructions		10
V.	Employees Want Five Things		10
W.	Some Don'ts in Regard to Praise		11
X.	How to Gain Your Workers' Confidence		11
Y.	Sources of Employee Problems		11
Z.	The Supervisor's Key to Discipline		11
AA.	Five Important Processes of Management		12
BB.	When the Supervisor Fails to Plan		12
CC.	Fourteen General Principles of Management		12
DD.	Change		12
II.	Brief Topical Summaries		13
	A.	Who/What is the Supervisor?	13
	B.	The Sociology of Work	13
	C.	Principles and Practices of Supervision	14
	D.	Dynamic Leadership	14
	E.	Processes for Solving Problems	15
	F.	Training for Results	15
	G.	Health, Safety, and Accident Prevention	16
	H.	Equal Employment Opportunity	16
	I.	Improving Communications	16
	J.	Self-Development	17
	K.	Teaching and Training	17
		1. The Teaching Process	17
		a. Preparation	17
		b. Presentation	18
		c. Summary	18
		d. Application	18
		e. Evaluation	18
		2. Teaching Methods	18
		a. Lecture	18
		b. Discussion	18
		c. Demonstration	19
		d. Performance	19
		e. Which Method to Use	19

PHILOSOPHY, PRINCIPLES, PRACTICES, AND TECHNICS
OF
SUPERVISION, ADMINISTRATION, MANAGEMENT, AND ORGANIZATION

MEANING OF SUPERVISION

The extension of the democratic philosophy has been accompanied by an extension in the scope of supervision. Modern leaders and supervisors no longer think of supervision in the narrow sense of being confined chiefly to visiting employees, supplying materials, or rating the staff. They regard supervision as being intimately related to all the concerned agencies of society, they speak of the supervisor's function in terms of "growth," rather than the "improvement" of employees.

This modern concept of supervision may be defined as follows: Supervision is leadership and the development of leadership within groups which are cooperatively engaged in inspection, research, training, guidance, and evaluation.

THE OLD AND THE NEW SUPERVISION

TRADITIONAL
1. Inspection
2. Focused on the employee
3. Visitation
4. Random and haphazard
5. Imposed and authoritarian
6. One person usually

MODERN
1. Study and analysis
2. Focused on aims, materials, methods, supervisors, employees, environment
3. Demonstrations, intervisitation, workshops, directed reading, bulletins, etc.
4. Definitely organized and planned (scientific)
5. Cooperative and democratic
6. Many persons involved (creative)

THE EIGHT (8) BASIC PRINCIPLES OF THE NEW SUPERVISION

I. Principle of Responsibility
   Authority to act and responsibility for acting must be joined.
   A. If you give responsibility, give authority.
   B. Define employee duties clearly.
   C. Protect employees from criticism by others.
   D. Recognize the rights as well as obligations of employees.
   E. Achieve the aims of a democratic society insofar as it is possible within the area of your work.
   F. Establish a situation favorable to training and learning.
   G. Accept ultimate responsibility for everything done in your section, unit, office, division, department.
   H. Good administration and good supervision are inseparable.

II. Principle of Authority
The success of the supervisor is measured by the extent to which the power of authority is not used.
- A. Exercise simplicity and informality in supervision
- B. Use the simplest machinery of supervision
- C. If it is good for the organization as a whole, it is probably justified.
- D. Seldom be arbitrary or authoritative.
- E. Do not base your work on the power of position or of personality.
- F. Permit and encourage the free expression of opinions.

III. Principle of Self-Growth
The success of the supervisor is measured by the extent to which, and the speed with which, he is no longer needed.
- A. Base criticism on principles, not on specifics.
- B. Point out higher activities to employees.
- C. Train for self-thinking by employees to meet new situations.
- D. Stimulate initiative, self-reliance, and individual responsibility
- E. Concentrate on stimulating the growth of employees rather than on removing defects.

IV. Principle of Individual Worth
Respect for the individual is a paramount consideration in supervision.
- A. Be human and sympathetic in dealing with employees.
- B. Don't nag about things to be done.
- C. Recognize the individual differences among employees and seek opportunities to permit best expression of each personality.

V. Principle of Creative Leadership
The best supervision is that which is not apparent to the employee.
- A. Stimulate, don't drive employees to creative action.
- B. Emphasize doing good things.
- C. Encourage employees to do what they do best.
- D. Do not be too greatly concerned with details of subject or method.
- E. Do not be concerned exclusively with immediate problems and activities.
- F. Reveal higher activities and make them both desired and maximally possible.
- G. Determine procedures in the light of each situation but see that these are derived from a sound basic philosophy.
- H. Aid, inspire, and lead so as to liberate the creative spirit latent in all good employees.

VI. Principle of Success and Failure
There are no unsuccessful employees, only unsuccessful supervisors who have failed to give proper leadership.
- A. Adapt suggestions to the capacities, attitudes, and prejudices of employees.
- B. Be gradual, be progressive, be persistent.
- C. Help the employee find the general principle; have the employee apply his own problem to the general principle.
- D. Give adequate appreciation for good work and honest effort.
- E. Anticipate employee difficulties and help to prevent them.
- F. Encourage employees to do the desirable things they will do anyway.
- G. Judge your supervision by the results it secures.

VII. Principle of Science
Successful supervision is scientific, objective, and experimental. It is based on facts, not on prejudices.
   A. Be cumulative in results.
   B. Never divorce your suggestions from the goals of training.
   C. Don't be impatient of results.
   D. Keep all matters on a professional, not a personal, level.
   E. Do not be concerned exclusively with immediate problems and activities.
   F. Use objective means of determining achievement and rating where possible.

VIII. Principle of Cooperation
Supervision is a cooperative enterprise between supervisor and employee.
   A. Begin with conditions as they are.
   B. Ask opinions of all involved when formulating policies.
   C. Organization is as good as its weakest link.
   D. Let employees help to determine policies and department programs.
   E. Be approachable and accessible—physically and mentally.
   F. Develop pleasant social relationships.

WHAT IS ADMINISTRATION

Administration is concerned with providing the environment, the material facilities, and the operational procedures that will promote the maximum growth and development of supervisors and employees. (Organization is an aspect and a concomitant of administration.)

There is no sharp line of demarcation between supervision and administration; these functions are intimately interrelated and, often, overlapping. They are complementary activities.

I. Practices Commonly Classed as "Supervisory"
   A. Conducting employees' conferences
   B. Visiting sections, units, offices, divisions, departments
   C. Arranging for demonstrations
   D. Examining plans
   E. Suggesting professional reading
   F. Interpreting bulletins
   G. Recommending in-service training courses
   H. Encouraging experimentation
   I. Appraising employee morale
   J. Providing for intervisitation

II. Practices Commonly Classified as "Administrative"
   A. Management of the office
   B. Arrangement of schedules for extra duties
   C. Assignment of rooms or areas
   D. Distribution of supplies
   E. Keeping records and reports
   F. Care of audio-visual materials
   G. Keeping inventory records
   H. Checking record cards and books

      I. Programming special activities
      J. Checking on the attendance and punctuality of employees

III. Practices Commonly Classified as Both "Supervisory" and "Administrative"
    A. Program construction
    B. Testing or evaluating outcomes
    C. Personnel accounting
    D. Ordering instructional materials

RESPONSIBILITIES OF THE SUPERVISOR

A person employed in a supervisory capacity must constantly be able to improve his own efficiency and ability. He represent the employer to the employees and only continuous self-examination can make him a capable supervisor.

Leadership and training are the supervisor's responsibility. An efficient working unit is one in which the employees work with the supervisor. It is his job to bring out the best in his employees. He must always be relaxed, courteous, and calm in his association with his employees. Their feelings are important, and a harsh attitude does not develop the most efficient employees.

COMPETENCES OF THE SUPERVISOR

    I. Complete knowledge of the duties and responsibilities of his position.
    II. To be able to organize a job, plan ahead, and carry through.
    III. To have self-confidence and initiative.
    IV. To be able to handle the unexpected situation and make quick decisions.
    V. To be able to properly train subordinates in the positions they are best suited for.
    VI. To be able to keep good human relations among his subordinates.
    VII. To be able to keep good human relations between his subordinates and himself and to earn their respect and trust.

THE PROFESSIONAL SUPERVISOR-EMPLOYEE RELATIONSHIP

There are two kinds of efficiency: one kind is only apparent and is produced in organizations through the exercise of mere discipline; this is but a simulation of the second, or true, efficiency which springs from spontaneous cooperation. If you are a manager, no matter how great or small your responsibility, it is your job, in the final analysis, to create and develop this involuntary cooperation among the people whom you supervise. For, no matter how powerful a combination of money, machines, and materials a company may have, this is a dead and sterile thing without a team of willing, thinking, and articulate people to guide it.

The following 21 points are presented as indicative of the exemplary basic relationship that should exist between supervisor and employee:

1. Each person wants to be liked and respected by his fellow employee and wants to be treated with consideration and respect by his superior.
2. The most competent employee will make an error. However, in a unit where good relations exist between the supervisor and his employees, tenseness and fear do not exist. Thus, errors are not hidden or covered up, and the efficiency of a unit is not impaired.

3. Subordinates resent rules, regulations, or orders that are unreasonable or unexplained.
4. Subordinates are quick to resent unfairness, harshness, injustices, and favoritism.
5. An employee will accept responsibility if he knows that he will be complimented for a job well done, and not too harshly chastised for failure; that his supervisor will check the cause of the failure, and, if it was the supervisor's fault, he will assume the blame therefore. If it was the employee's fault, his supervisor will explain the correct method or means of handling the responsibility.
6. An employee wants to receive credit for a suggestion he has made, that is used. If a suggestion cannot be used, the employee is entitled to an explanation. The supervisor should not say "no" and close the subject.
7. Fear and worry slow up a worker's ability. Poor working environment can impair his physical and mental health. A good supervisor avoids forceful methods, threats, and arguments to get a job done.
8. A forceful supervisor is able to train his employees individually and as a team, and is able to motivate them in the proper channels.
9. A mature supervisor is able to properly evaluate his subordinates and to keep them happy and satisfied.
10. A sensitive supervisor will never patronize his subordinates.
11. A worthy supervisor will respect his employees' confidences.
12. Definite and clear-cut responsibilities should be assigned to each executive.
13. Responsibility should always be coupled with corresponding authority.
14. No change should be made in the scope or responsibilities of a position without a definite understanding to that effect on the part of all persons concerned.
15. No executive or employee, occupying a single position in the organization, should be subject to definite orders from more than one source.
16. Orders should never be given to subordinates over the head of a responsible executive. Rather than do this, the officer in question should be supplanted.
17. Criticisms of subordinates should, whoever possible, be made privately, and in no case should a subordinate be criticized in the presence of executives or employees of equal or lower rank.
18. No dispute or difference between executives or employees as to authority or responsibilities should be considered too trivial for prompt and careful adjudication.
19. Promotions, wage changes, and disciplinary action should always be approved by the executive immediately superior to the one directly responsible.
20. No executive or employee should ever be required, or expected, to be at the same time an assistant to, and critic of, another.
21. Any executive whose work is subject to regular inspection should, wherever practicable, be given the assistance and facilities necessary to enable him to maintain an independent check of the quality of his work.

MINI-TEXT IN SUPERVISION, ADMINISTRATION, MANAGEMENT, AND ORGANIZATION

I. Brief Highlights

Listed concisely and sequentially are major headings and important data in the field for quick recall and review.

A. Levels of Management
Any organization of some size has several levels of management. In terms of a ladder, the levels are:

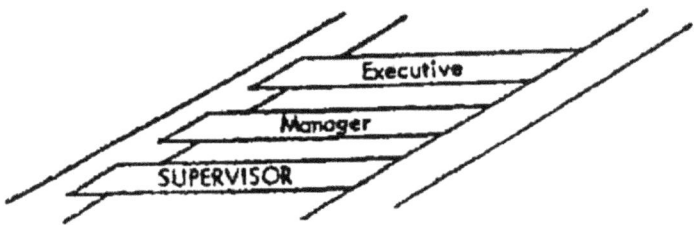

The first level is very important because it is the beginning point of management leadership.

B. What the Supervisor Must Learn
A supervisor must learn to:
1. Deal with people and their differences
2. Get the job done through people
3. Recognize the problems when they exist
4. Overcome obstacles to good performance
5. Evaluate the performance of people
6. Check his own performance in terms of accomplishment

C. A Definition of Supervisor
The term supervisor means any individual having authority, in the interests of the employer, to hire, transfer, suspend, lay-off, recall, promote, discharge, assign, reward, or discipline other employees or responsibility to direct them, or to adjust their grievances, or effectively to recommend such action, if, in connection with the foregoing, exercise of such authority is not of a merely routine or clerical nature but requires the use of independent judgment.

D. Elements of the Team Concept
What is involved in teamwork? The component parts are:
1. Members
2. A leader
3. Goals
4. Plans
5. Cooperation
6. Spirit

E. Principles of Organization
1. A team member must know what his job is.
2. Be sure that the nature and scope of a job are understood.
3. Authority and responsibility should be carefully spelled out.
4. A supervisor should be permitted to make the maximum number of decisions affecting his employees.
5. Employees should report to only one supervisor.
6. A supervisor should direct only as many employees as he can handle effectively.
7. An organization plan should be flexible.

8. Inspection and performance of work should be separate.
9. Organizational problems should receive immediate attention.
10. Assign work in line with ability and experience.

F. The Four Important Parts of Every Job
1. Inherent in every job is the *accountability* for results.
2. A second set of factors in every job is *responsibilities*.
3. Along with duties and responsibilities one must have the *authority* to act within certain limits without obtaining permission to proceed.
4. No job exists in a vacuum. The supervisor is surrounded by key *relationships*.

G. Principles of Delegation
Where work is delegated for the first time, the supervisor should think in terms of these questions:
1. Who is best qualified to do this?
2. Can an employee improve his abilities by doing this?
3. How long should an employee spend on this?
4. Are there any special problems for which he will need guidance?
5. How broad a delegation can I make?

H. Principles of Effective Communications
1. Determine the media.
2. To whom directed?
3. Identification and source authority.
4. Is communication understood?

I. Principles of Work Improvement
1. Most people usually do only the work which is assigned to them.
2. Workers are likely to fit assigned work into the time available to perform it.
3. A good workload usually stimulates output.
4. People usually do their best work when they know that results will be reviewed or inspected.
5. Employees usually feel that someone else is responsible for conditions of work, workplace layout, job methods, type of tools/equipment, and other such factors.
6. Employees are usually defensive about their job security.
7. Employees have natural resistance to change.
8. Employees can support or destroy a supervisor.
9. A supervisor usually earns the respect of his people through his personal example of diligence and efficiency.

J. Areas of Job Improvement
The areas of job improvement are quite numerous, but the most common ones which a supervisor can identify and utilize are:
1. Departmental layout
2. Flow of work
3. Workplace layout
4. Utilization of manpower
5. Work methods
6. Materials handling

7. Utilization
8. Motion economy

K. Seven Key Points in Making Improvements
1. Select the job to be improved
2. Study how it is being done now
3. Question the present method
4. Determine actions to be taken
5. Chart proposed method
6. Get approval and apply
7. Solicit worker participation

L. Corrective Techniques of Job Improvement
Specific Problems
1. Size of workload
2. Inability to meet schedules
3. Strain and fatigue
4. Improper use of men and skills
5. Waste, poor quality, unsafe conditions
6. Bottleneck conditions that hinder output
7. Poor utilization of equipment and machine
8. Efficiency and productivity of labor

General Improvement
1. Departmental layout
2. Flow of work
3. Work plan layout
4. Utilization of manpower
5. Work methods
6. Materials handling
7. Utilization of equipment
8. Motion economy

Corrective Techniques
1. Study with scale model
2. Flow chart study
3. Motion analysis
4. Comparison of units produced to standard allowance
5. Methods analysis
6. Flow chart and equipment study
7. Down time vs. running time
8. Motion analysis

M. A Planning Checklist
1. Objectives
2. Controls
3. Delegations
4. Communications
5. Resources
6. Manpower

7. Equipment
8. Supplies and materials
9. Utilization of time
10. Safety
11. Money
12. Work
13. Timing of improvements

N. Five Characteristics of Good Directions
In order to get results, directions must be:
1. Possible of accomplishment
2. Agreeable with worker interests
3. Related to mission
4. Planned and complete
5. Unmistakably clear

O. Types of Directions
1. Demands or direct orders
2. Requests
3. Suggestion or implication
4. volunteering

P. Controls
A typical listing of the overall areas in which the supervisor should establish controls might be:
1. Manpower
2. Materials
3. Quality of work
4. Quantity of work
5. Time
6. Space
7. Money
8. Methods

Q. Orienting the New Employee
1. Prepare for him
2. Welcome the new employee
3. Orientation for the job
4. Follow-up

R. Checklist for Orienting New Employees   Yes   No
1. Do you appreciate the feelings of new employees
   when they first report for work?   ___   ___
2. Are you aware of the fact that the new employee must
   make a big adjustment to his job?   ___   ___
3. Have you given him good reasons for liking the job and
   the organization?   ___   ___
4. Have you prepared for his first day on the job?   ___   ___
5. Did you welcome him cordially and make him feel needed?   ___   ___

			Yes	No
	6.	Did you establish rapport with him so that he feels free to talk and discuss matters with you?	___	___
	7.	Did you explain his job to him and his relationship to you?	___	___
	8.	Does he know that his work will be evaluated periodically on a basis that is fair and objective?	___	___
	9.	Did you introduce him to his fellow workers in such a way that they are likely to accept him?	___	___
	10.	Does he know what employee benefits he will receive?	___	___
	11.	Does he understand the importance of being on the job and what to do if he must leave his duty station?	___	___
	12.	Has he been impressed with the importance of accident prevention and safe practice?	___	___
	13.	Does he generally know his way around the department?	___	___
	14.	Is he under the guidance of a sponsor who will teach the right way of doing things?	___	___
	15.	Do you plan to follow-up so that he will continue to adjust successfully to his job?	___	___

S. Principles of Learning
    1. Motivation
    2. Demonstration or explanation
    3. Practice

T. Causes of Poor Performance
    1. Improper training for job
    2. Wrong tools
    3. Inadequate directions
    4. Lack of supervisory follow-up
    5. Poor communications
    6. Lack of standards of performance
    7. Wrong work habits
    8. Low morale
    9. Other

U. Four Major Steps in On-The-Job Instruction
    1. Prepare the worker
    2. Present the operation
    3. Tryout performance
    4. Follow-up

V. Employees Want Five Things
    1. Security
    2. Opportunity
    3. Recognition
    4. Inclusion
    5. Expression

W. Some Don'ts in Regard to Praise
   1. Don't praise a person for something he hasn't done.
   2. Don't praise a person unless you can be sincere.
   3. Don't be sparing in praise just because your superior withholds it from you.
   4. Don't let too much time elapse between good performance and recognition of it

X. How to Gain Your Workers' Confidence
   Methods of developing confidence include such things as:
   1. Knowing the interests, habits, hobbies of employees
   2. Admitting your own inadequacies
   3. Sharing and telling of confidence in others
   4. Supporting people when they are in trouble
   5. Delegating matters that can be well handled
   6. Being frank and straightforward about problems and working conditions
   7. Encouraging others to bring their problems to you
   8. Taking action on problems which impede worker progress

Y. Sources of Employee Problems
   On-the-job causes might be such things as:
   1. A feeling that favoritism is exercised in assignments
   2. Assignment of overtime
   3. An undue amount of supervision
   4. Changing methods or systems
   5. Stealing of ideas or trade secrets
   6. Lack of interest in job
   7. Threat of reduction in force
   8. Ignorance or lack of communications
   9. Poor equipment
   10. Lack of knowing how supervisor feels toward employee
   11. Shift assignments

   Off-the-job problems might have to do with:
   1. Health
   2. Finances
   3. Housing
   4. Family

Z. The Supervisor's Key to Discipline
   There are several key points about discipline which the supervisor should keep in mind:
   1. Job discipline is one of the disciplines of life and is directed by the supervisor.
   2. It is more important to correct an employee fault than to fix blame for it.
   3. Employee performance is affected by problems both on the job and off.
   4. Sudden or abrupt changes in behavior can be indications of important employee problems.
   5. Problems should be dealt with as soon as possible after they are identified.
   6. The attitude of the supervisor may have more to do with solving problems than the techniques of problem solving.
   7. Correction of employee behavior should be resorted to only after the supervisor is sure that training or counseling will not be helpful.

8. Be sure to document your disciplinary actions.
9. Make sure that you are disciplining on the basis of facts rather than personal feelings.
10. Take each disciplinary step in order, being careful not to make snap judgments, or decisions based on impatience.

AA. Five Important Processes of Management
1. Planning
2. Organizing
3. Scheduling
4. Controlling
5. Motivating

BB. When the Supervisor Fails to Plan
1. Supervisor creates impression of not knowing his job
2. May lead to excessive overtime
3. Job runs itself—supervisor lacks control
4. Deadlines and appointments missed
5. Parts of the work go undone
6. Work interrupted by emergencies
7. Sets a bad example
8. Uneven workload creates peaks and valleys
9. Too much time on minor details at expense of more important tasks

CC. Fourteen General Principles of Management
1. Division of work
2. Authority and responsibility
3. Discipline
4. Unity of command
5. Unity of direction
6. Subordination of individual interest to general interest
7. Remuneration of personnel
8. Centralization
9. Scalar chain
10. Order
11. Equity
12. Stability of tenure of personnel
13. Initiative
14. Esprit de corps

DD. Change

Bringing about change is perhaps attempted more often, and yet less well understood, than anything else the supervisor does. How do people generally react to change? (People tend to resist change that is imposed upon them by other individuals or circumstances.

Change is characteristic of every situation. It is a part of every real endeavor where the efforts of people are concerned.

1. Why do people resist change?
   People may resist change because of:
   a. Fear of the unknown
   b. Implied criticism
   c. Unpleasant experiences in the past
   d. Fear of loss of status
   e. Threat to the ego
   f. Fear of loss of economic stability

2. How can we best overcome the resistance to change?
   In initiating change, take these steps:
   a. Get ready to sell
   b. Identify sources of help
   c. Anticipate objections
   d. Sell benefits
   e. Listen in depth
   f. Follow up

II. Brief Topical Summaries

   A. Who/What is the Supervisor?
      1. The supervisor is often called the "highest level employee and the lowest level manager."
      2. A supervisor is a member of both management and the work group. He acts as a bridge between the two.
      3. Most problems in supervision are in the area of human relations, or people problems.
      4. Employees expect: Respect, opportunity to learn and to advance, and a sense of belonging, and so forth.
      5. Supervisors are responsible for directing people and organizing work. Planning is of paramount importance.
      6. A position description is a set of duties and responsibilities inherent to a given position.
      7. It is important to keep the position description up-to-date and to provide each employee with his own copy.

   B. The Sociology of Work
      1. People are alike in many ways; however, each individual is unique.
      2. The supervisor is challenged in getting to know employee differences. Acquiring skills in evaluating individuals is an asset.
      3. Maintaining meaningful working relationships in the organization is of great importance.
      4. The supervisor has an obligation to help individuals to develop to their fullest potential.
      5. Job rotation on a planned basis helps to build versatility and to maintain interest and enthusiasm in work groups.
      6. Cross training (job rotation) provides backup skills.

7. The supervisor can help reduce tension by maintaining a sense of humor, providing guidance to employees, and by making reasonable and timely decisions. Employees respond favorably to working under reasonably predictable circumstances.
8. Change is characteristic of all managerial behavior. The supervisor must adjust to changes in procedures, new methods, technological changes, and to a number of new and sometimes challenging situations.
9. To overcome the natural tendency for people to resist change, the supervisor should become more skillful in initiating change.

C. Principles and Practices of Supervision
1. Employees should be required to answer to only one superior.
2. A supervisor can effectively direct only a limited number of employees, depending upon the complexity, variety, and proximity of the jobs involved.
3. The organizational chart presents the organization in graphic form. It reflects lines of authority and responsibility as well as interrelationships of units within the organization.
4. Distribution of work can be improved through an analysis using the "Work Distribution Chart."
5. The "Work Distribution Chart" reflects the division of work within a unit in understandable form.
6. When related tasks are given to an employee, he has a better chance of increasing his skills through training.
7. The individual who is given the responsibility for tasks must also be given the appropriate authority to insure adequate results.
8. The supervisor should delegate repetitive, routine work. Preparation of recurring reports, maintaining leave and attendance records are some examples.
9. Good discipline is essential to good task performance. Discipline is reflected in the actions of employees on the job in the absence of supervision.
10. Disciplinary action may have to be taken when the positive aspects of discipline have failed. Reprimand, warning, and suspension are examples of disciplinary action.
11. If a situation calls for a reprimand, be sure it is deserved and remember it is to be done in private.

D. Dynamic Leadership
1. A style is a personal method or manner of exerting influence.
2. Authoritarian leaders often see themselves as the source of power and authority.
3. The democratic leader often perceives the group as the source of authority and power.
4. Supervisors tend to do better when using the pattern of leadership that is most natural for them.
5. Social scientists suggest that the effective supervisor use the leadership style that best fits the problem or circumstances involved.
6. All four styles—telling, selling, consulting, joining—have their place. Using one does not preclude using the other at another time.

7. The theory X point of view assumes that the average person dislikes work, will avoid it whenever possible, and must be coerced to achieve organizational objectives.
8. The theory Y point of view assumes that the average person considers work to be a natural as play, and, when the individual is committed, he requires little supervision or direction to accomplish desired objectives.
9. The leader's basic assumptions concerning human behavior and human nature affect his actions, decisions, and other managerial practices.
10. Dissatisfaction among employees is often present, but difficult to isolate. The supervisor should seek to weaken dissatisfaction by keeping promises, being sincere and considerate, keeping employees informed, and so forth.
11. Constructive suggestions should be encouraged during the natural progress of the work.

E. Processes for Solving Problems
1. People find their daily tasks more meaningful and satisfying when they can improve them.
2. The causes of problems, or the key factors, are often hidden in the background. Ability to solve problems often involves the ability to isolate them from their backgrounds. There is some substance to the cliché that some persons "can't see the forest for the trees."
3. New procedures are often developed from old ones. Problems should be broken down into manageable parts. New ideas can be adapted from old one.
4. People think differently in problem-solving situations. Using a logical, patterned approach is often useful. One approach found to be useful includes these steps:
   a. Define the problem
   b. Establish objectives
   c. Get the facts
   d. Weigh and decide
   e. Take action
   f. Evaluate action

F. Training for Results
1. Participants respond best when they feel training is important to them.
2. The supervisor has responsibility for the training and development of those who report to him.
3. When training is delegated to others, great care must be exercised to insure the trainer has knowledge, aptitude, and interest for his work as a trainer.
4. Training (learning) of some type goes on continually. The most successful supervisor makes certain the learning contributes in a productive manner to operational goals.
5. New employees are particularly susceptible to training. Older employees facing new job situations require specific training, as well as having need for development and growth opportunities.
6. Training needs require continuous monitoring.
7. The training officer of an agency is a professional with a responsibility to assist supervisors in solving training problems.

8. Many of the self-development steps important to the supervisor's own growth are equally important to the development of peers and subordinates. Knowledge of these is important when the supervisor consults with others on development and growth opportunities.

G. Health, Safety, and Accident Prevention
1. Management-minded supervisors take appropriate measures to assist employees in maintaining health and in assuring safe practices in the work environment.
2. Effective safety training and practices help to avoid injury and accidents.
3. Safety should be a management goal. All infractions of safety which are observed should be corrected without exception.
4. Employees' safety attitude, training and instruction, provision of safe tools and equipment, supervision, and leadership are considered highly important factors which contribute to safety and which can be influenced directly by supervisors.
5. When accidents do occur, they should be investigated promptly for very important reasons, including the fact that information which is gained can be used to prevent accidents in the future.

H. Equal Employment Opportunity
1. The supervisor should endeavor to treat all employees fairly, without regard to religion, race, sex, or national origin.
2. Groups tend to reflect the attitude of the leader. Prejudice can be detected even in very subtle form. Supervisors must strive to create a feeling of mutual respect and confidence in every employee.
3. Complete utilization of all human resources is a national goal. Equitable consideration should be accorded women in the work force, minority-group members, the physically and mentally handicapped, and the older employee. The important question is: "Who can do the job?"
4. Training opportunities, recognition for performance, overtime assignments, promotional opportunities, and all other personnel actions are to be handled on an equitable basis.

I. Improving Communications
1. Communications is achieving understanding between the sender and the receiver of a message. It also means sharing information—the creation of understanding.
2. Communication is basic to all human activity. Words are means of conveying meanings; however, real meanings are in people.
3. There are very practical differences in the effectiveness of one-way, impersonal, and two-way communications. Words spoken face-to-face are better understood. Telephone conversations are effective, but lack the rapport of person-to-person exchanges. The whole person communicates.
4. Cooperation and communication in an organization go hand in hand. When there is a mutual respect between people, spelling out rules and procedures for communicating is unnecessary.
5. There are several barriers to effective communications. These include failure to listen with respect and understanding, lack of skill in feedback, and misinterpreting the meanings of words used by the speaker. It is also common

practice to listen to what we want to hear, and tune out things we do not want to hear.
6. Communication is management's chief problem. The supervisor should accept the challenge to communicate more effectively and to improve interagency and intra-agency communications.
7. The supervisor may often plan for and conduct meetings. The planning phase is critical and may determine the success or the failure of a meeting.
8. Speaking before groups usually requires extra effort. Stage fright may never disappear completely, but it can be controlled.

J. Self-Development
1. Every employee is responsible for his own self-development.
2. Toastmaster and toastmistress clubs offer opportunities to improve skills in oral communications.
3. Planning for one's own self-development is of vital importance. Supervisors know their own strengths and limitations better than anyone else.
4. Many opportunities are open to aid the supervisor in his developmental efforts, including job assignments; training opportunities, both governmental and non-governmental—to include universities and professional conferences and seminars.
5. Programmed instruction offers a means of studying at one's own rate.
6. Where difficulties may arise from a supervisor's being away from his work for training, he may participate in televised home study or correspondence courses to meet his self-development needs.

K. Teaching and Training
1. The Teaching Process
Teaching is encouraging and guiding the learning activities of students toward established goals. In most cases this process consists of five steps: preparation, presentation, summarization, evaluation, and application.

   a. Preparation
   Preparation is two-fold in nature; that of the supervisor and the employee. Preparation by the supervisor is absolutely essential to success. He must know what, when, where, how, and whom he will teach. Some of the factors that should be considered are:
   1) The objectives
   2) The materials needed
   3) The methods to be used
   4) Employee participation
   5) Employee interest
   6) Training aids
   7) Evaluation
   8) Summarization

   Employee preparation consists in preparing the employee to receive the material. Probably the most important single factor in the preparation of the employee is arousing and maintaining his interest. He must know the objectives of the training, why he is there, how the material can be used, and its importance to him.

b. Presentation
  In presentation, have a carefully designed plan and follow it. The plan should be accurate and complete, yet flexible enough to meet situations as they arise. The method of presentation will be determined by the particular situation and objectives.

c. Summary
  A summary should be made at the end of every training unit and program. In addition, there may be internal summaries depending on the nature of the material being taught. The important thing is that the trainee must always be able to understand how each part of the new material relates to the whole.

d. Application
  The supervisor must arrange work so the employee will be given a chance to apply new knowledge or skills while the material is still clear in his mind and interest is high. The trainee does not really know whether he has learned the material until he has been given a chance to apply it. If the material is not applied, it loses most of its value.

e. Evaluation
  The purpose of all training is to promote learning. To determine whether the training has been a success or failure, the supervisor must evaluate this learning.
  In the broadest sense, evaluation includes all the devices, methods, skills, and techniques used by the supervisor to keep himself and the employees informed as to their progress toward the objectives they are pursuing. The extent to which the employee has mastered the knowledge, skills, and abilities, or changed his attitudes, as determined by the program objectives, is the extent to which instruction has succeeded or failed.
  Evaluation should not be confined to the end of the lesson, day, or program but should be used continuously. We shall note later the way this relates to the rest of the teaching process.

2. Teaching Methods
  A teaching method is a pattern of identifiable student and instructor activity used in presenting training material.
  All supervisors are faced with the problem of deciding which method should be used at a given time.

  a. Lecture
    The lecture is direct oral presentation of material by the supervisor. The present trend is to place less emphasis on the trainer's activity and more on that of the trainee.

  b. Discussion
    Teaching by discussion or conference involves using questions and other techniques to arouse interest and focus attention upon certain areas, and by doing so creating a learning situation. This can be one of the most

valuable methods because it gives the employees an opportunity to express their ideas and pool their knowledge.

c. Demonstration
The demonstration is used to teach how something works or how to do something. It can be used to show a principle or what the results of a series of actions will be. A well-staged demonstration is particularly effective because it shows proper methods of performance in a realistic manner.

d. Performance
Performance is one of the most fundamental of all learning techniques or teaching methods. The trainee may be able to tell how a specific operation should be performed but he cannot be sure he knows how to perform the operation until he has done so.
As with all methods, there are certain advantages and disadvantages to each method.

e. Which Method to Use
Moreover, there are other methods and techniques of teaching. It is difficult to use any method without other methods entering into it. In any learning situation, a combination of methods is usually more effective than any one method alone.

Finally, evaluation must be integrated into the other aspects of the teaching-learning process.

It must be used in the motivation of the trainees; it must be used to assist in developing understanding during the training; and it must be related to employee application of the results of training.

This is distinctly the role of the supervisor.

BASIC FUNDAMENTALS OF
DRAWINGS AND SPECIFICATIONS

A building project may be broadly divided into two major phases: (1) the DESIGN phase, and (2) the CONSTRUCTION phase. In accordance with a number of considerations, of which the function and desired appearance of the building are perhaps the most important, the architect first conceives the building in his mind's eye, as it were, and then sets his concept down on paper in the form of PRESENTATION drawings. Presentation drawings are usually done in PERSPECTIVE, by employing the PICTORIAL drawing techniques.

Next the architect and the engineer, working together, decide upon the materials to be used in the structure and the construction methods which are to be followed. The engineer determines the loads which supporting members will carry and the strength qualities the members must have to bear the loads. He also designs the mechanical systems of the structure, such as the lighting, heating, and plumbing systems. The end-result of all this is the preparation of architectural and engineering DESIGN SKETCHES. The purpose of these sketches is to guide draftsmen in the preparation of CONSTRUCTION DRAWINGS.

The construction drawings, plus the SPECIFICATIONS to be described later, are the chief sources of information for the supervisors and craftsman responsible for the actual work of construction. Construction drawings consist mostly of ORTHOGRAPHIC views, prepared by draftsmen who employ the standard technical drawing techniques, and who use the symbols and other designations

You should make a thorough study of symbols before proceeding further with this chapter. Figure 1 illustrates the conventional symbols for the more common types of material used on structures. Figure 2 shows the more common symbols used for doors and windows.

Before you can interpret construction drawings correctly, you must also have some knowledge of the structure and of the terminology for common structural members.

I. STRUCTURES

The main parts of a structure are the LOAD-BEARING STRUCTURAL MEMBERS, which support and transfer the loads on the structure while remaining in equilibrium with each other. The places where members are connected to other members are called JOINTS. The sum total of the load supported by the structural members at a particular instant is equal to the total DEAD LOAD plus the total LIVE LOAD.

The total dead load is the total weight of the structure, which gradually increases, of course, as the structure rises, and remains constant once it is completed. The total live load is the total weight of movable objects (such as people, furniture, bridge traffic or the like) which the structure happens to be supporting at a particular instant.

The live loads in a structure are transmitted through the various load-bearing structural members to the ultimate support of the earth as follows. Immediate or direct support for the live loads is provided by HORIZTONAL members; these are in turn supported by VERTICAL members; which in turn are supported by FOUNDATIONS and/or FOOTINGS; and these are, finally, supported by the earth.

The ability of the earth to support a load is called the SOIL BEARING CAPACITY; it is determined by test and measured in pounds per square foot. Soil bearing capacity varies considerably with different types of soil, and a soil of given bearing capacity will bear a heavier load on a wide foundation or footing than it will on a narrow one.

VERTICAL STRUCTURAL MEMBERS

Vertical structural members are high-strength columns; they are sometimes called PILLARS in buildings. Outside wall columns and inside bottom-floor columns, usually rest directly on footings. Outside-wall columns usually extend from the footing or foundation to the roof line. Inside bottom-floor columns extend upward from footings or foundations to horizontal members which in turn support the

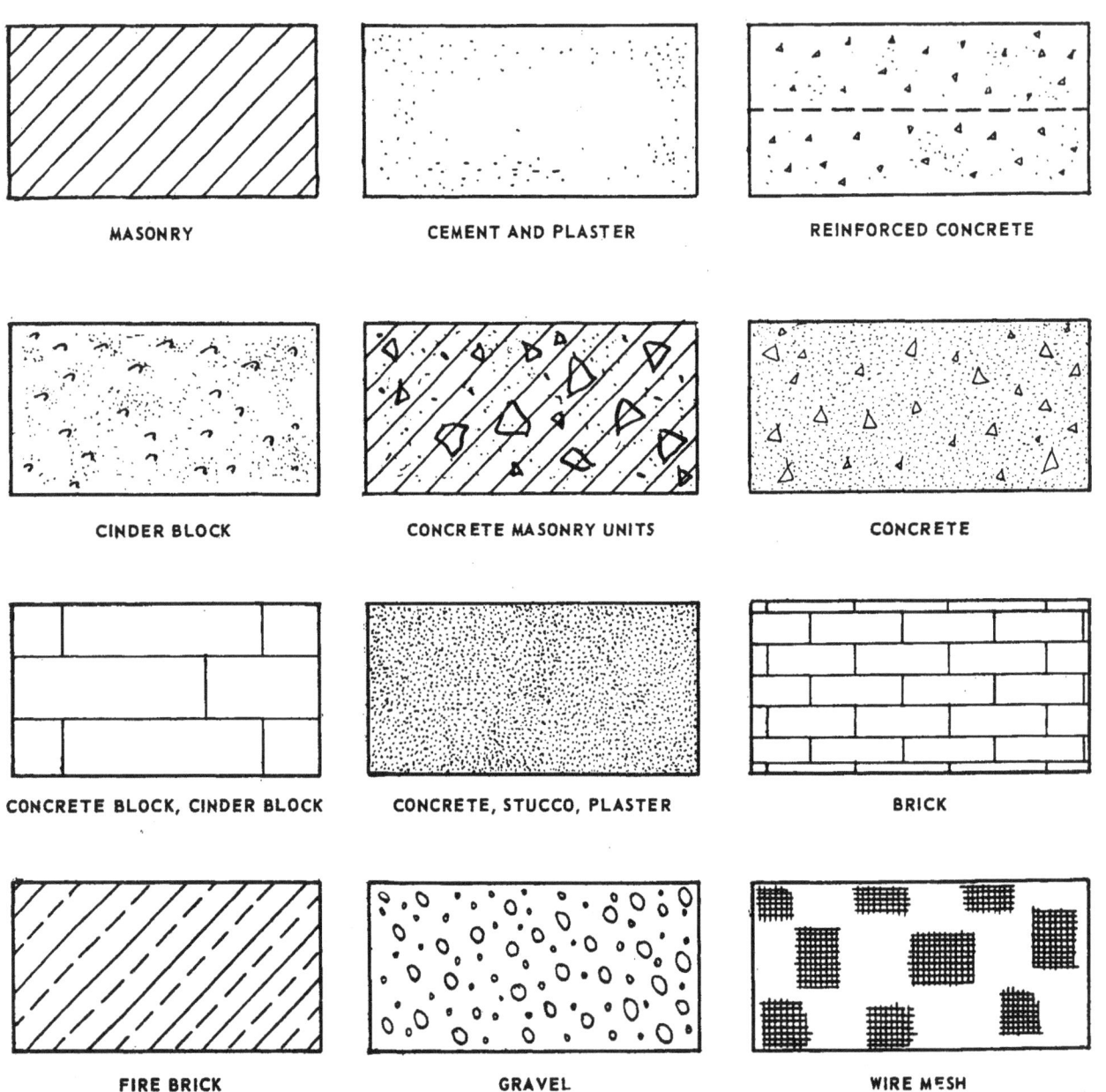

Figure 1.—Material symbols.

first floor. Upper floor columns usually are located directly over lower floor columns.

A PIER in building construction might be called a short column. It may rest directly on a footing, or it may be simply set or driven in the ground. Building piers usually support the lowermost horizontal structural members.

In bridge construction a pier is a vertical member which provides intermediate support for the bridge superstructure.

The chief vertical structural members in light frame construction are called STUDS. They are supported on horizontal members called SILLS or SOLE PLATES, and are topped by horizontal members called TOP PLATES or RAFTER PLATES. CORNER POSTS are enlarged studs, as it were, located at the building corners. In early FULL-FRAME construction a corner post was usually a solid piece of larger timber. In most modern construction BUILT-UP

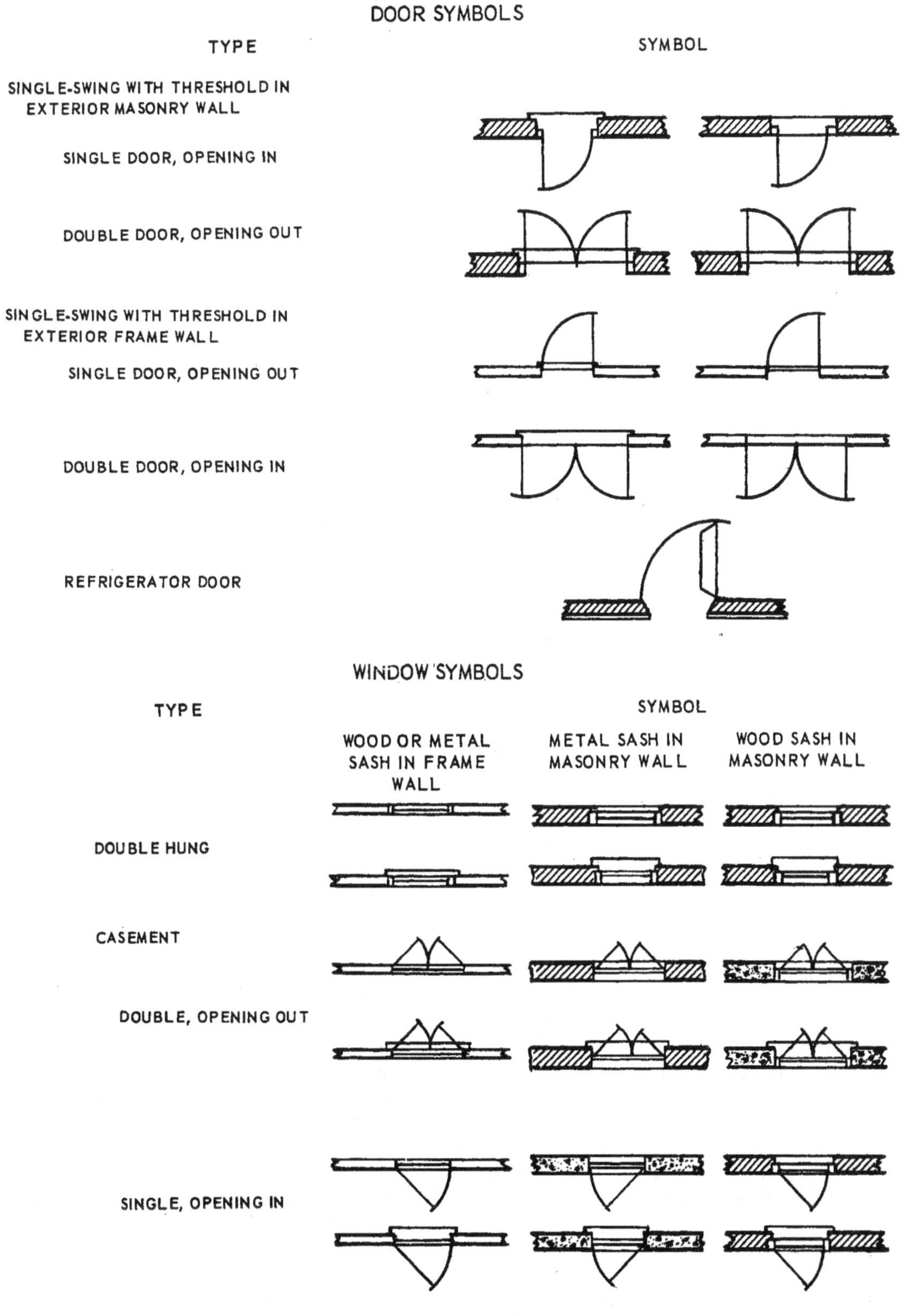

DOOR SYMBOLS

TYPE	SYMBOL
SINGLE-SWING WITH THRESHOLD IN EXTERIOR MASONRY WALL SINGLE DOOR, OPENING IN	
DOUBLE DOOR, OPENING OUT	
SINGLE-SWING WITH THRESHOLD IN EXTERIOR FRAME WALL SINGLE DOOR, OPENING OUT	
DOUBLE DOOR, OPENING IN	
REFRIGERATOR DOOR	

WINDOW SYMBOLS

TYPE	WOOD OR METAL SASH IN FRAME WALL	METAL SASH IN MASONRY WALL	WOOD SASH IN MASONRY WALL
DOUBLE HUNG			
CASEMENT DOUBLE, OPENING OUT			
SINGLE, OPENING IN			

Figure 2 —Architectural symbols (door and windows).

corner posts are used, consisting of various numbers of ordinary studs, nailed together in various ways.

HORIZONTAL STRUCTURAL MEMBERS

In technical terminology, a horizontal load-bearing structural member which spans a space, and which is supported at both ends, is called a BEAM. A member which is FIXED at one end only is called a CANTILEVER. Steel members which consist of solid pieces of the regular structural steel shapes are called beams, but a type of steel member which is actually a light truss is called an OPEN-WEB STEEL JOIST or a BAR STEEL JOIST.

Horizontal structural members which support the ends of floor beams or joists in wood frame construction are called SILLS, GIRTS, or GIRDERS, depending on the type of framing being done and the location of the member in the structure. Horizontal members which support studs are called SILL or SOLE PLATES. Horizontal members which support the wall-ends of rafters are called RAFTER PLATES. Horizontal members which assume the weight of concrete or masonry walls above door and window openings are called LINTELS.

TRUSSES

A beam of given strength, without intermediate supports below, can support a given load over only a certain maximum span. If the span is wider than this maximum, intermediate supports, such as a column must be provided for the beam. Sometimes it is not feasible or possible to install intermediate supports. When such is the case, a TRUSS may be used instead of a beam.

A beam consists of a single horizontal member. A truss, however, is a framework, consisting of two horizontal (or nearly horizontal) members, joined together by a number of vertical and/or inclined members. The horizontal members are called the UPPER and LOWER CHORDS; the vertical and/or inclined members are called the WEB MEMBERS.

ROOF MEMBERS

The horizontal or inclined members which provide support to a roof are called RAFTERS. The lengthwise (right angle to the rafters) member which support the peak ends of the rafters in a roof is called the RIDGE. (The ridge may be called the Ridge board, the Ridge PIECE, or the Ridge pole.) Lengthwise members other than ridges are called PURLINS. In wood frame construction the wall ends of rafters are supported on horizontal members called RAFTER PLATES, which are in turn supported by the outside wall studs. In concrete or masonry wall construction, the wall ends of rafters may be anchored directly on the walls, or on plates bolted to the walls.

II. CONSTRUCTION DRAWINGS

Construction drawings are drawings in which as much construction information as possible is presented GRAPHICALLY, or by means of pictures. Most construction drawings consist of ORTHOGRAPHIC views. GENERAL drawings consist of PLANS AND ELEVATIONS, drawn on a relatively small scale. DETAIL drawings consist of SECTIONS and DETAILS, drawn on a relatively large scale.

PLANS

A PLAN view is, as you know, a view of an object or area as it would appear if projected onto a horizontal plane passed through or held above the object or area. The most common construction plans are PLOT PLANS (also called SITE PLANS), FOUNDATION PLANS, FLOOR PLANS, and FRAMING PLANS.

A PLOT PLAN shows the contours, boundaries, roads, utilities, trees, structures, and any other significant physical features pertaining to or located on the site. The locations of proposed structures are indicated by appropriate outlines or floor plans. By locating the corners of a proposed structure at given distances from a REFERENCE or BASE line (which is shown on the plan and which can be located on the site), the plot plan provides essential data for those who will lay out the building lines. By indicating the elevations of existing and proposed earth surfaces (by means of CONTOUR lines), the plot plan provides essential data for the graders and excavators.

A FOUNDATION PLAN (fig. 3) is a plan view of a structure projected on a horizontal plane passed through (in imagination, of course) at the level of the tops of the foundations. The plan shown in figure 3 tells you that the main foundation of this structure will consist of a rectangular 12-in. concrete block wall, 22 ft

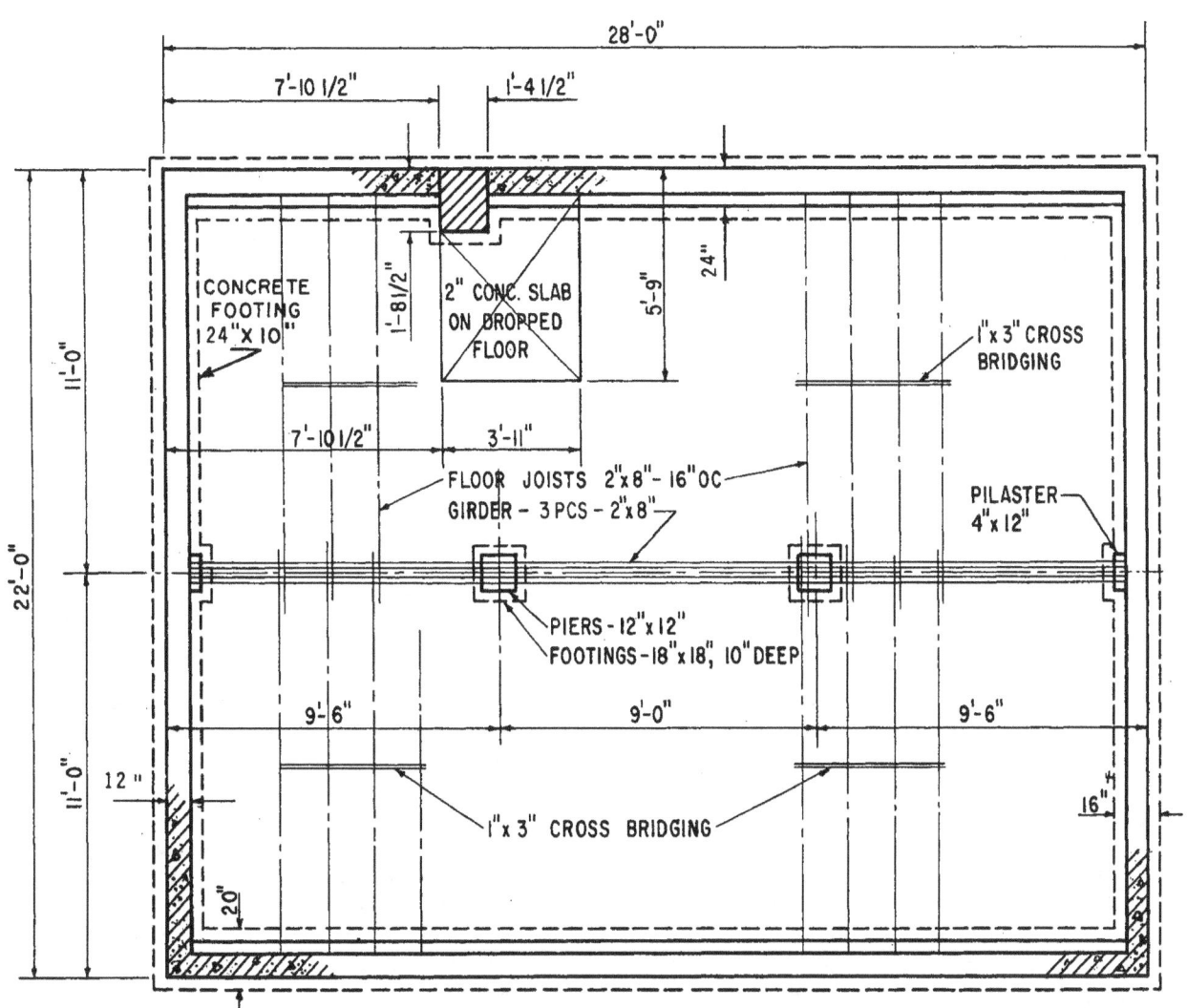

Figure 3.—Foundation plan.

wide by 28 ft long, centered on a concrete footing 24 in. wide. Besides the outside wall and footing, there will be two 12-in. square piers, centered on 18-in. square footings, and located on center 9 ft 6 in. from the end wall building lines. These piers will support a ground floor center-line girder.

A FLOOR PLAN (also called a BUILDING PLAN) is developed as shown in figure 4. Information on a floor plan includes the lengths, thicknesses, and character of the building walls at that particular floor, the widths and locations of door and window openings, the lengths and character of partitions, the number and arrangement of rooms, and the types and locations of utility installations. A typical floor plan is shown in figure 5.

FRAMING PLANS show the dimensions, numbers, and arrangement of structural members in wood frame construction. A simple FLOOR FRAMING PLAN is superimposed on the foundation plan shown in figure 3. From this foundation plan you learn that the ground-floor joists in this structure will consist of 2 x 8's, lapped at the girder, and spaced 16 in. O. C. The plan also shows that each row of joists is to be braced by a row of 1 x 3 cross bridging. For a more complicated floor framing problem, a framing plan like the one shown in figure 2-6 would be required. This plan

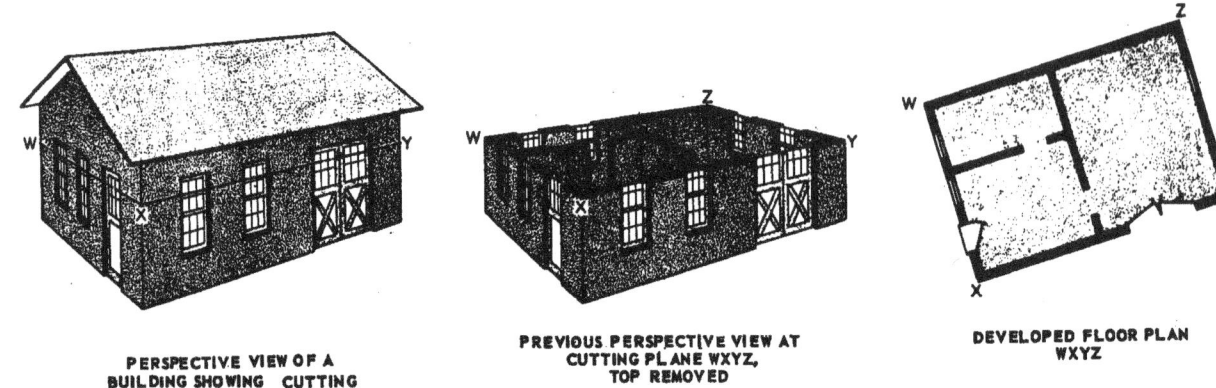

Figure 4.—Floor plan development.

shows, among other things, the arrangement of joists and other members around stair wells and other floor openings.

A WALL FRAMING PLAN gives similar information with regard to the studs, corner posts, bracing, sills, plates, and other structural members in the walls. Since it is a view on a vertical plane, a wall framing plan is not a plan in the strict technical sense. However, the practice of calling it a plan has become a general custom. A ROOF FRAMING PLAN gives similar information with regard to the rafters, ridge, purlins, and other structural members in the roof.

A UTILITY PLAN is a floor plan which shows the layout of a heating, electrical, plumbing, or other utility system. Utility plans are used primarily by the ratings responsible for the utilities, but they are important to the Builder as well. Most utility installations require the leaving of openings in walls, floors, and roofs for the admission or installation of utility features. The Builder who is placing a concrete foundation wall must study the utility plans to determine the number, sizes, and locations of the openings he must leave for utilities.

Figure 7 shows a heating plan. Figure 8 shows an electrical plan.

ELEVATIONS

ELEVATIONS show the front, rear, and sides of a structure projected on vertical planes parallel to the planes of the sides. Front, rear, right side, and left side elevations of a small building are shown in figure 9.

As you can see, the elevations give you a number of important vertical dimensions, such as the perpendicular distance from the finish floor to the top of the rafter plate and from the finish floor to the tops of door and window finished openings. They also show the locations and characters of doors and windows. Dimensions of window sash and dimensions and character of lintels, however, are usually set forth in a WINDOW SCHEDULE.

A SECTION view is a view of a cross-section, developed as indicated in figure 10. By general custom, the term is confined to views of cross-sections cut by vertical planes. A floor plan or foundation plan, cut by a horizontal plane, is, technically speaking, a section view as well as a plan view, but it is seldom called a section.

The most important sections are the WALL sections. Figure 11 shows three wall sections for three alternate types of construction for the building shown in figures 3, 5, 7 and 8. The angled arrows marked "A" in figure 5 indicate the location of the cutting plane for the sections.

The wall sections are of primary importance to the supervisors of construction and to the craftsmen who will do the actual building. Take the first wall section, marked "masonry construction," for example. Starting at the bottom, you learn that the footing will be concrete, 2 ft wide and 10 in. high. The vertical distance of the bottom of the footing below FINISHED GRADE (level of the finished earth surface around the house) "varies"—meaning that it will depend on the soil-bearing capacity at the particular site. The foundation wall will consist of

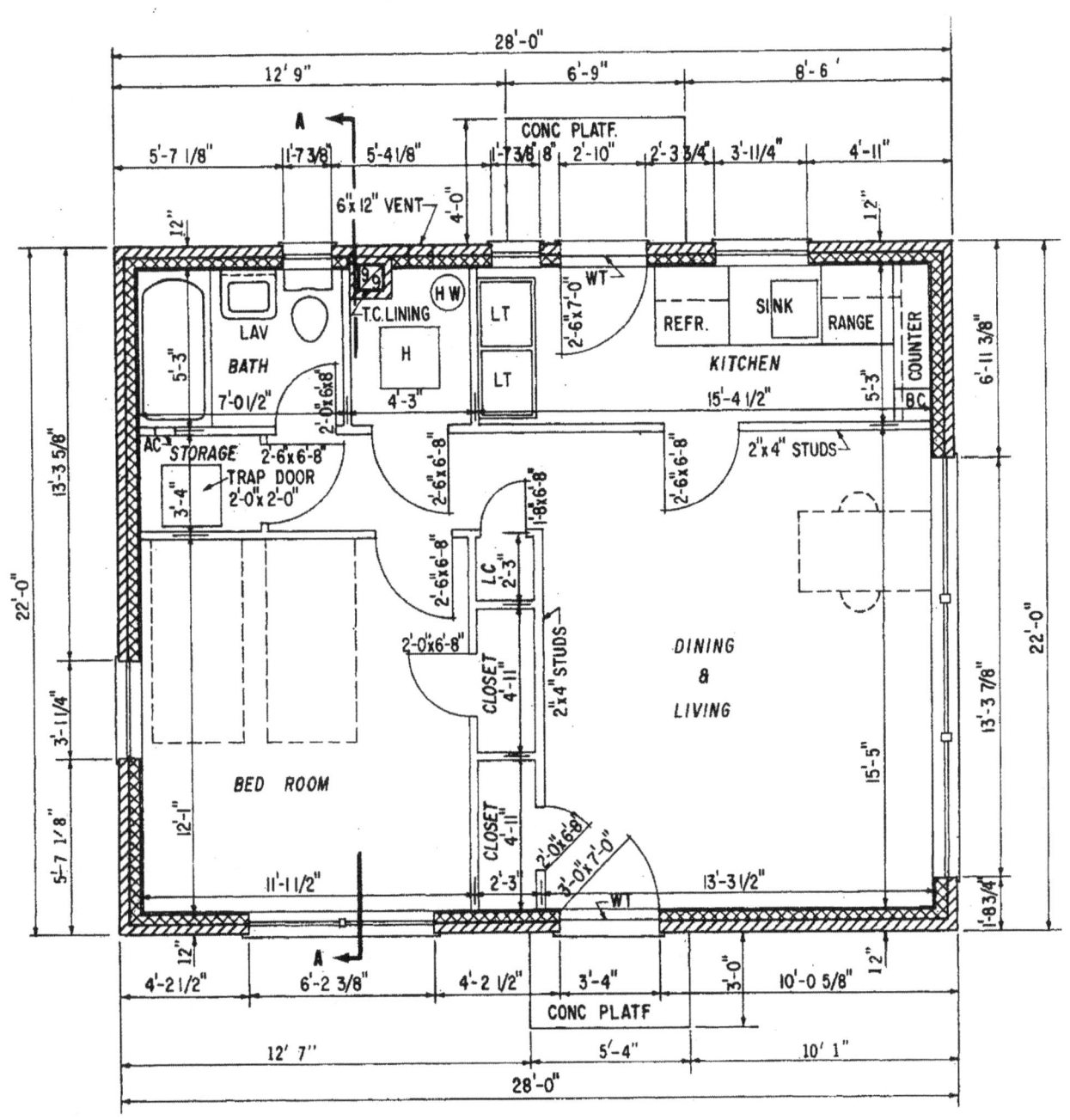

Figure 5.—Floor plan.

12-in. CMU, centered on the footing. Twelve-inch blocks will extend up to an unspecified distance below grade, where a 4-in. brick FACING (dimension indicated in the middle wall section) begins. Above the line of the bottom of the facing, it is obvious that 8-in. instead of 12-in. blocks will be used in the foundation wall.

The building wall above grade will consist of a 4-in. brick FACING TIER, backed by a BACKING TIER of 4-in. cinder blocks. The floor joists, consisting of 2 x 8's placed 16 in. O.C., will be anchored on 2 x 4 sills bolted to the top of the foundation wall. Every third joist will be additionally secured by a 2 x 1/4 STRAP ANCHOR embedded in the cinder block backing tier of the building wall.

The window (window B in the plan front elevation, fig. 9) will have a finished opening

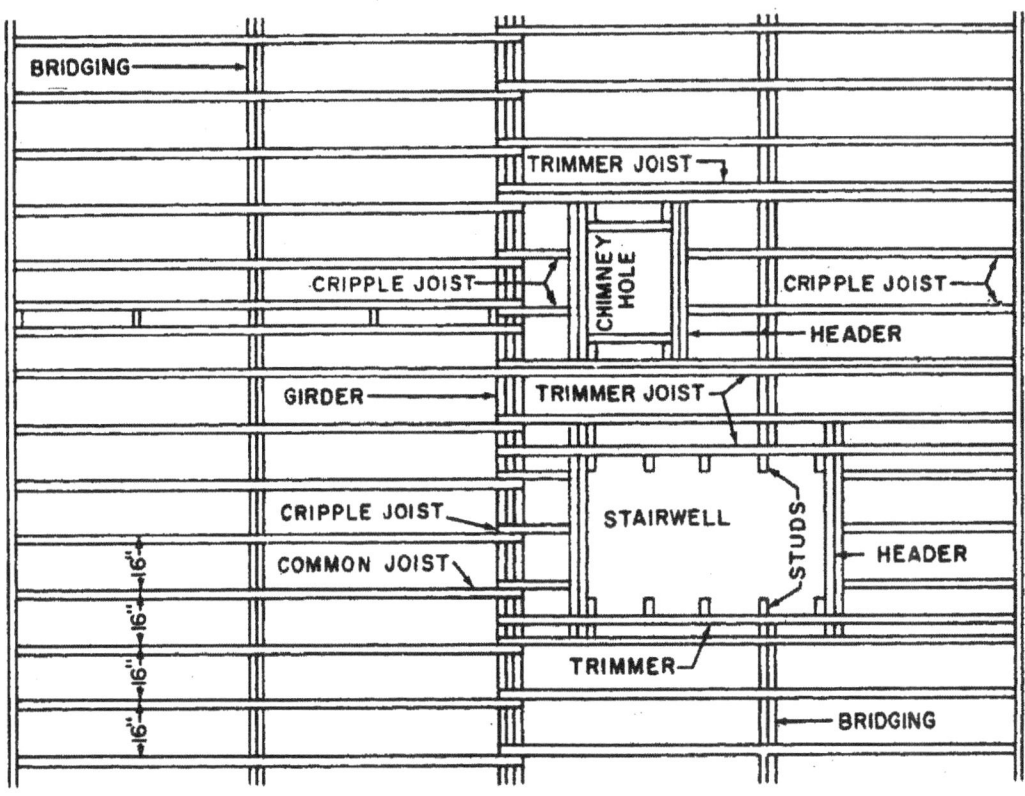

Figure 6.—Floor framing plan.

4 ft 2-5/8 in. high. The bottom of the opening will come 2 ft 11-3/4 in. above the line of the finished floor. As indicated in the wall section, (fig. 11) 13 masonry COURSES (layers of masonry units) above the finished floor line will amount to a vertical distance of 2 ft 11-3/4 in. As also indicated, another 19 courses will amount to the prescribed vertical dimension of the finished window opening.

Window framing details, including the placement and cross-sectional character of the lintel, are shown. The building wall will be carried 10-1/4 in., less the thickness of a 2 x 8 RAFTER PLATE, above the top of the window finished opening. The total vertical distance from the top of the finished floor to the top of the rafter plate will be 8 ft 2-1/4 in. Ceiling joists and rafters will consist of 2 x 6's, and the roof covering will consist of composition shingles laid on wood sheathing.

Flooring will consist of a wood finisher floor laid on a wood subfloor. Inside walls will be finished with plaster on lath (except on masonry wall which would be with or without lath as directed). A minimum of 2 vertical feet of crawl space will extend below the bottoms of the floor joists.

The middle wall section in figure 2-11 gives you similar information for a similar building constructed with wood frame walls and a DOUBLE-HUNG window. The third wall section shown in the figure gives you similar information for a similar building constructed with a steel frame, a casement window, and a concrete floor finished with asphalt tile.

DETAILS

DETAIL drawings are drawings which are done on a larger scale than that of the general drawings, and which show features not appearing at all, or appearing on too small a scale, on the general drawings. The wall sections just described are details as well as sections, since

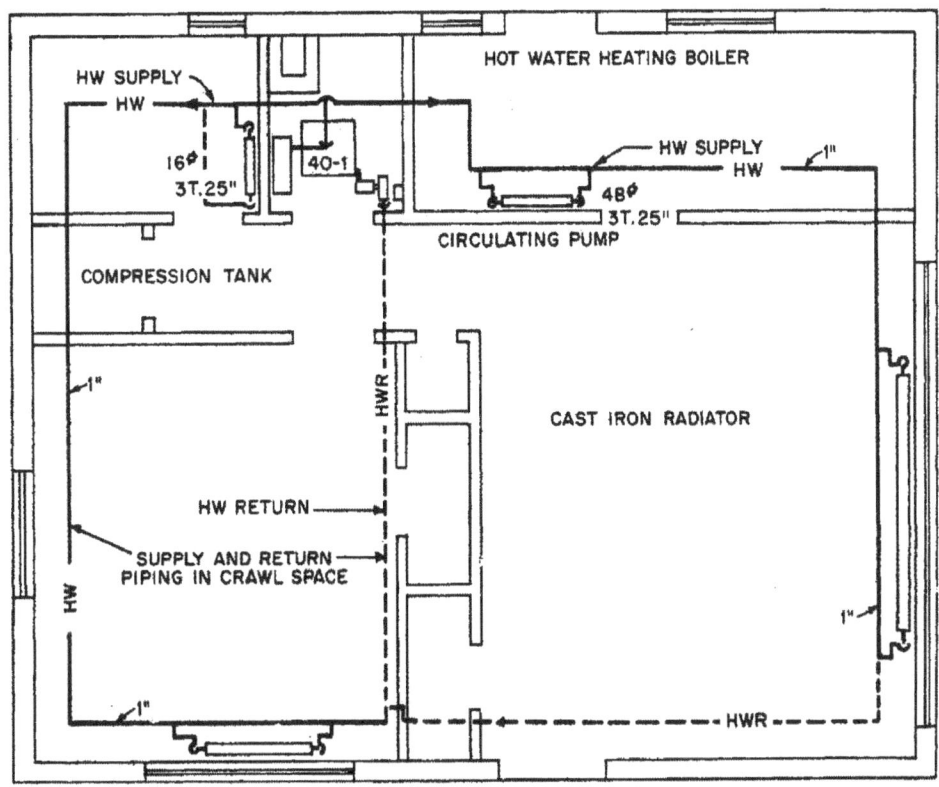

Figure 7.—Heating plan.

they are drawn on a considerable larger scale than the plans and elevations. Framing details at doors, windows, and cornices, which are the most common types of details, are practically always sections.

Details are included whenever the information given in the plans, elevations, and wall sections is not sufficiently "detailed" to guide the craftsmen on the job. Figure 12 shows some typical door and window wood framing details, and an eave detail for a very simple type of CORNICE. You should study these details closely to learn the terminology of framing members.

III. SPECIFICATIONS

The construction drawings contain much of the information about a structure which can be presented GRAPHICALLY (that is, in drawings). A very considerable amount of information can be presented this way, but there is more information which the construction supervisors and artisans must have and which is not adaptable to the graphic form of presentation. Information of this kind includes quality criteria for materials (maximum amounts of aggregate per sack of cement, for example), specified standards of workmanship, prescribed construction methods, and the like.

Information of this kind is presented in a list of written SPECIFICATIONS, familiarly known as the "SPECS." A list of specifications usually begins with a section on GENERAL CONDITIONS. This section starts with a GENERAL DESCRIPTION of the building, including the type of foundation, type or types of windows, character of framing, utilities to be installed, and the like. Next comes a list of DEFINITIONS of terms used in the specs, and next certain routine declarations of responsibility and certain conditions to be maintained on the job.

SPECIFIC CONDITIONS are grouped in sections under headings which describe each of the major construction phases of the job. Separate specifications are written for each phase, and the phases are then combined to more or less follow the usual order of construction sequences on the job. A typical list of sections under "Specific Conditions" follows:

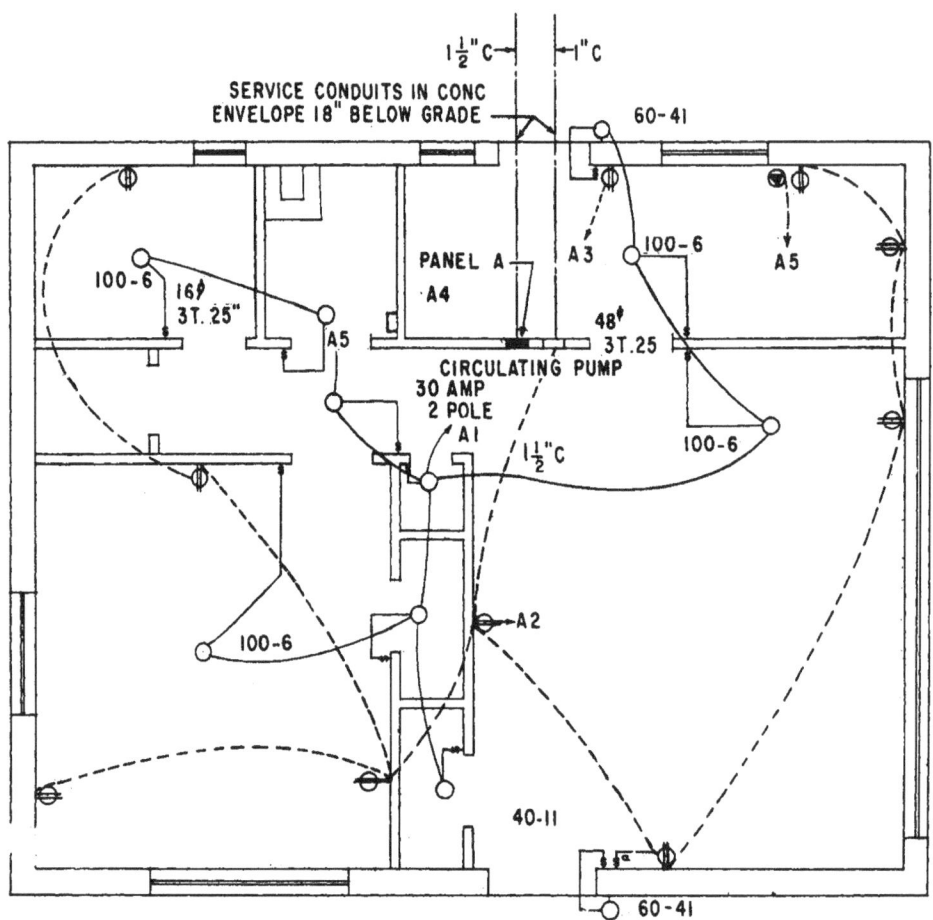

Figure 8.—Electrical plan.

2.—EARTHWORK 3.—CONCRETE 4.—MASONRY 5.—MISCELLANEOUS STEEL AND IRON 6.—CARPENTRY AND JOINERY 7.—LATHING AND PLASTERING 8.—TILE WORK 9.—FINISH FLOORING 10.—GLAZING 11.—FINISHING HARDWARE 12.—PLUMBING 13.—HEATING 14.—ELECTRICAL WORK 15.—FIELD PAINTING.

A section under "Specific Conditions" usually begins with a subsection of GENERAL REQUIREMENTS which apply to the phase of construction being considered. Under Section 6, CARPENTRY AND JOINERY, for example, the first section might go as follows:

6-01. GENERAL REQUIREMENTS. All framing, rough carpentry, and finishing woodwork required for the proper completion of the building shall be provided. All woodwork shall be protected from the weather, and the building shall be thoroughly dry before the finish is placed. All finish shall be dressed, smoothed, and sandpapered at the mill, and in addition shall be hand smoothed and sandpapered at the building where necessary to produce proper finish. Nailing shall be done, as far as practicable, in concealed places, and all nails in finishing work shall be set. All lumber shall be S4S (meaning, "surfaced on 4 sides"); all materials for millwork and finish shall be kiln-dried; all rough and framing lumber shall be air- or kiln-dried. Any cutting, fitting, framing, and blocking necessary for the accommodation of other work shall be provided. All nails, spikes, screws, bolts, plates, clips, and other fastenings and rough hardware necessary for the proper completion of the building shall be provided.

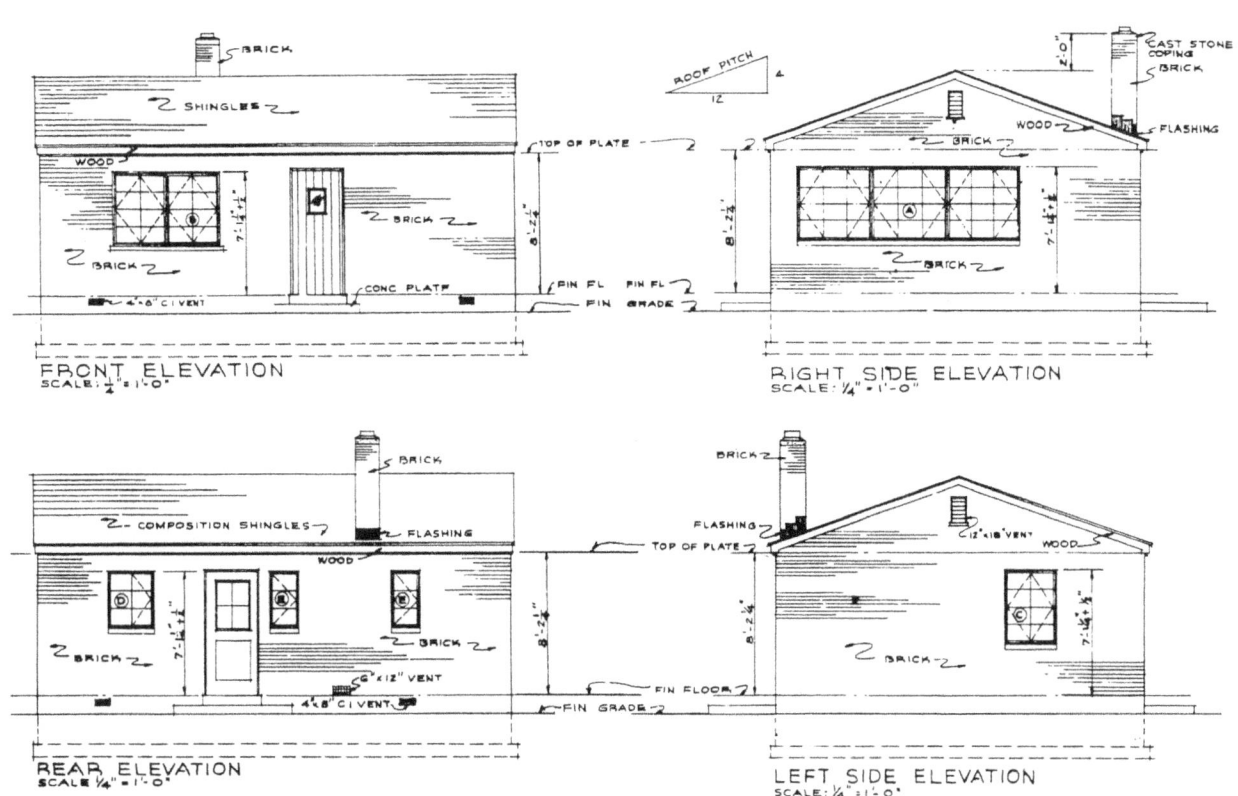

Figure 2-9.—Elevations.

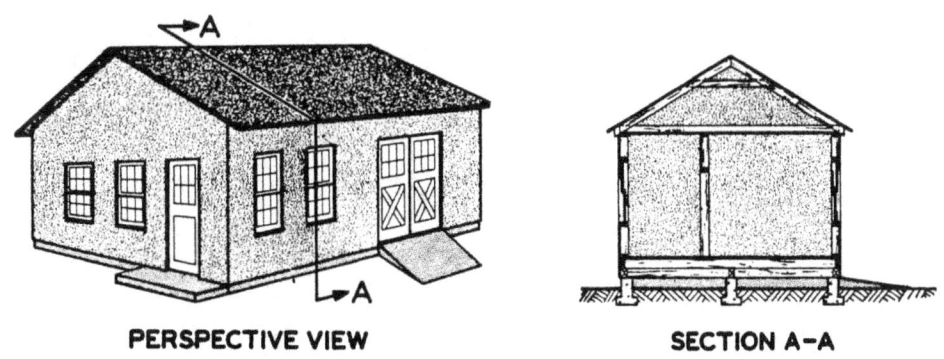

Figure 10.—Development of a section view.

All finishing hardware shall be installed in accordance with the manufacturers' directions. Calking and flashing shall be provided where indicated, or where necessary to provide weathertight construction.

Next after the General Requirements for Carpentry and Joinery, there is generally a subsection on "Grading," in which the kinds and grades of the various woods to be used in the structure are specified. Subsequent subsections

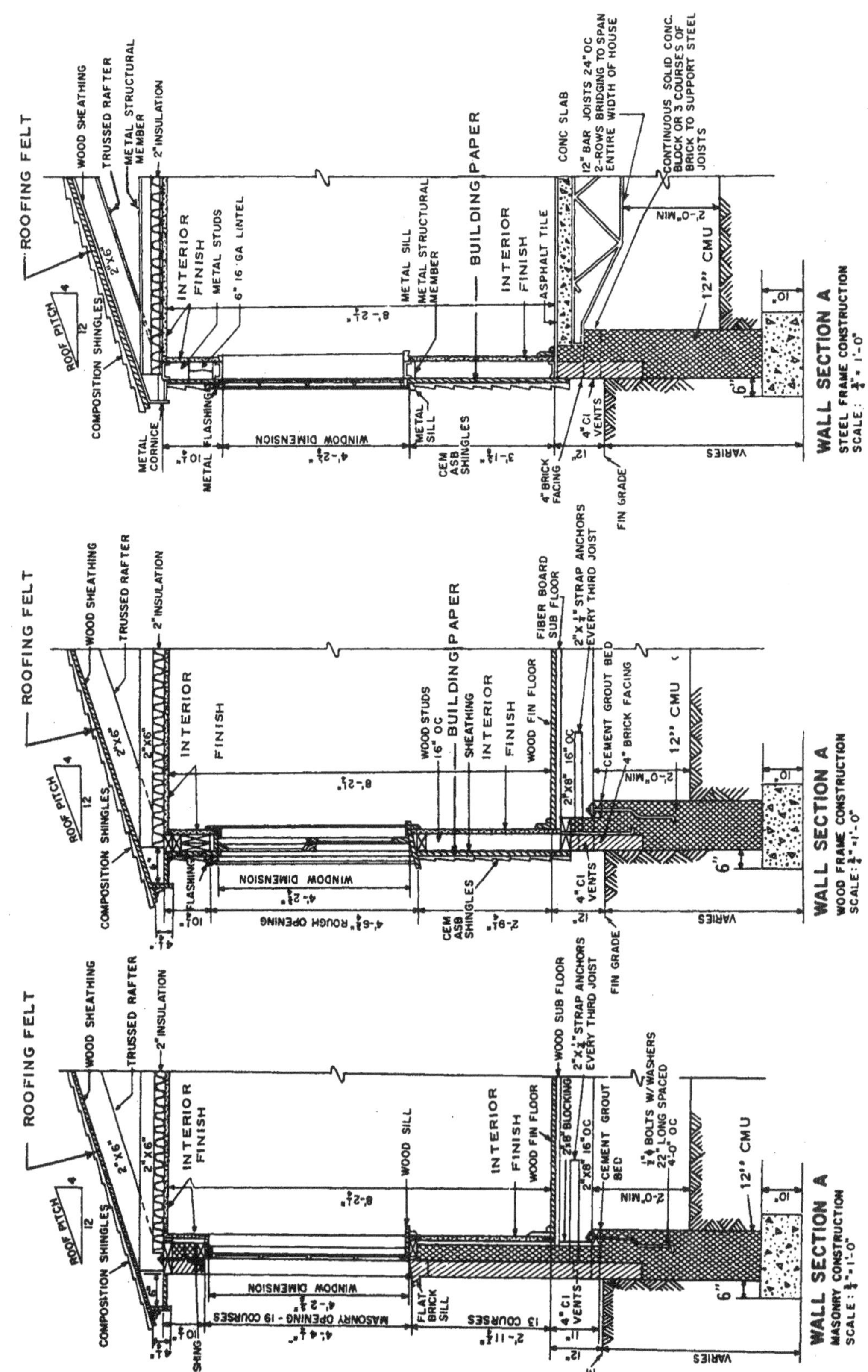

Figure 11.—Wall sections

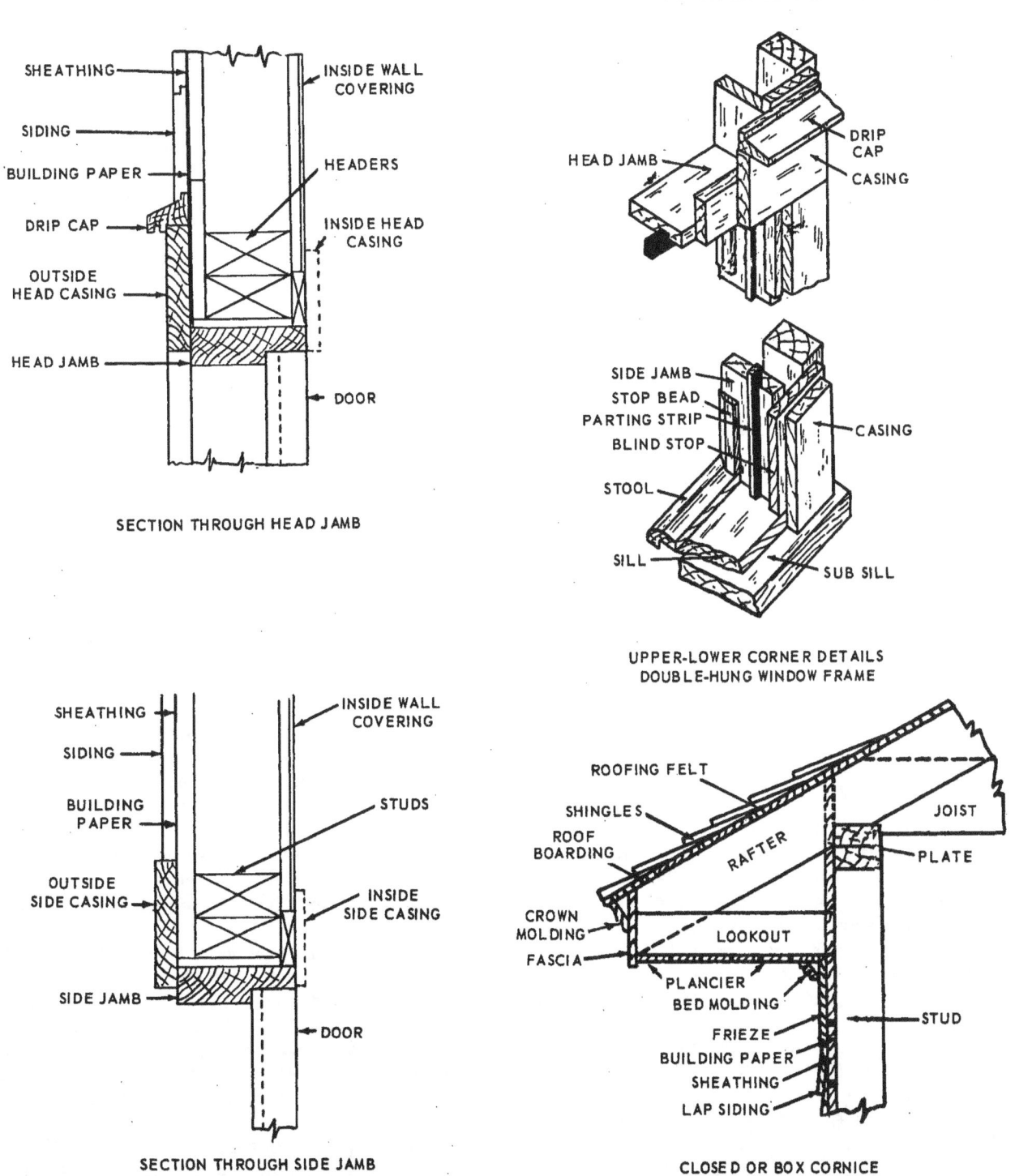

Figure 12.—Door, window and eave details.

specify various quality criteria and standards of workmanship for the various aspects of the rough and finish carpentry work, under such headings as FRAMING; SILLS, PLATES, AND GIRDERS; FLOOR JOISTS AND ROOF RAFTERS; STUDDING; and so on. An example of one of these subsections follows:

STUDDING for walls and partitions shall have doubled plates and doubled stud caps. Studs shall be set plumb and not to exceed 16-in. centers and in true alignment; they shall be bridged with one row of 2 x 4 pieces, set flatwise, fitted tightly, and nailed securely to each stud. Studding shall be doubled around openings and the heads of openings shall rest on the inner studs. Openings in partitions having widths of 4 ft and over shall be trussed. In wood frame construction, studs shall be trebled at corners to form posts.

From the above samples, you can see that a knowledge of the relevant specifications is as essential to the construction supervisor and the construction artisan as a knowledge of the construction drawings.

It is very important that the proper spec be used to cover the material requested. In cases in which the material is not covered by a Government spec, the ASTM (American Society for Testing Materials) spec or some other approved commercial spec may be used. It is EXTREMELY IMPORTANT in using specifications to cite all amendments, including the latest changes.

As a rule, the specs are provided for each project by the A/E (ARCHITECT-ENGINEERS). These are the OFFICIAL guidelines approved by the chief engineer or his representative for use during construction. These requirements should NOT be deviated from without prior approval from proper authority. This approval is usually obtained by means of a change order. When there is disagreement between the specifications and drawings, the specifications should normally be followed; however, check with higher authority in each case.

IV. BUILDER'S MATHEMATICS

The Builder has many occasions for the employment of the processes of ordinary arithmetic, and he must be thoroughly familiar with the methods of determining the areas and volumes of the various plane and solid geometrical figures. Only a few practical applications and a few practical suggestions, will be given here.

RATIO AND PROPORTION

There are a great many practical applications of ratio and proportion in the construction field. A few examples are as follows:

Some dimensions on construction drawings (such as, for example, distances from base lines and elevations of surfaces) are given in ENGINEER'S instead of CARPENTER's measure. Engineer's measure is measure in feet and decimal parts of a foot, or in inches and decimal parts of an inch, such as 100.15 ft or 11.14 in. Carpenter's measure is measure in yards, feet, inches, and even-denominator fractions of an inch, such as 1/2 in., 1/4 in., 1/16 in., 1/32 in., and 1/64 in.

You must know how to convert an engineer's measure given on a construction drawing to a carpenter's measure. Besides this, it will often happen that calculations you make yourself may produce a result in feet and decimal parts of a foot, which result you will have to convert to carpenter's measure. To convert engineer's to carpenter's measure you can use ratio and proportion as follows:

Let's say that you want to convert 100.14 ft to feet and inches to the nearest 1/16 in. The 100 you don't need to convert, since it is already in feet. What you need to do, first, is to find out how many twelfths of a foot (that is, how many inches) there are in 14/100 ft. Set this up as a proportional equation as follows: x:12::14:100.

You know that in a proportional equation the product of the means equals the product of the extremes. Consequently, 100x = (12 x 14), or 168. Then x = 168/100, or 1.68 in. Next question is, how many 16ths of an in. are there in 68/100 in.? Set this up, too, as a proportional equation, thus: x:16::68:100. Then 100x = 1088, and x = 10 88/100 sixteenths. Since 88/100 of a sixteenth is more than one-half of a sixteenth, you ROUND OFF by calling it 11/16. In 100.14 ft, then, there are 100 ft 1 11/16 in. For example:

A. $\underbrace{x:12::14:100}_{\text{Extremes}}$ means

Product of extremes = product of means:

$$100\ x = 168$$
$$x = 1.68\ \text{IN.}$$

B. x:16::68:100

$$100\ x = 1088$$

$$x = 10.88$$

$$x = 10\frac{88}{100}\ \text{sixteenths}$$

Rounded off to 11/16

Another way to convert engineer's measurements to carpenter's measurements is to multiply the decimal portion of a foot by 12 to get inches; multiply the decimal by 16 to get the fraction of an inch.

There are many other practical applications of ratio and proportion in the construction field. Suppose, for example, that a table tells you that, for the size and type of brick wall you happen to be laying, 12,321 bricks and 195 cu ft of mortar are required per every 1000 sq ft of wall. How many bricks and how much mortar will be needed for 750 sq ft of the same wall? You simply set up equations as follows; for example:

Brick: x:750::12,321:1000
Mortar: x:750::195:1000

Brick: $\frac{X}{750} = \frac{12,321}{1000}$ Cross multiply

$$1000\ X = 9,240,750\ \text{Divide}$$
$$X = 9,240.75 = 9241\ \text{Brick.}$$

Mortar: $\frac{X}{750} = \frac{195}{1000}$ Cross multiply

$$1000\ X = 146,250\ \text{Divide}$$
$$X = 146.25 = 146\ 1/4\ \text{cu ft}$$

Suppose, for another example, that the ingredient proportions by volume for the type of concrete you are making are 1 cu ft cement to 1.7 cu ft sand to 2.8 cu ft coarse aggregate. Suppose you know as well, by reference to a table, that ingredients combined in the amounts indicated will produce 4.07 cu ft of concrete. How much of each ingredient will be required to make a cu yd of concrete?

Remember here, first, that there are not 9, but 27 (3 ft x 3 ft x 3 ft) cu ft in a cu yd. Your proportional equations will be as follows:

Cement: x:27::1:4.07

Sand: x:27::1.7:4.07

Coarse aggregate: x:27::2.8:4.07

Cement: x:27::1:4.07

$$\frac{x}{27} = \frac{1}{4.07}$$

$$4.07\ x = 27$$

$$x = 6.63\ \text{cu ft Cement}$$

Sand: x:27::1.7:4.07

$$\frac{x}{27} = \frac{1.7}{4.07}$$

$$4.07\ x = 45.9$$

$$x = 11.28\ \text{cu ft Sand}$$

Coarse aggregate: x:27::2.8:407

$$\frac{x}{27} = \frac{2.8}{4.07}$$

$$4.07\ x = 75.6$$

$$x = 18.57\ \text{cu ft Coarse aggregate}$$

ARITHMETICAL OPERATIONS

The formulas for finding the area and volume of geometric figures are expressed in algebraic equations which are called formulas. A few of the more important formulas and their mathematical solutions will be discussed in this section.

DRAWINGS AND SPECIFICATIONS

To get an area, you multiply 2 linear measures together, and to get a volume you multiply 3 linear measures together. The linear measures you multiply together must all be expressed in the SAME UNITS; you cannot, for example, multiply a length in feet by a width in inches to get a result in square feet or in square inches.

Dimensions of a feature on a construction drawing are not always given in the same units. For a concrete wall, for example, the length and height are usually given in feet and the thickness in inches. Furthermore, you may want to get a result in units which are different from any shown on the drawing. Concrete volume, for example, is usually expressed in cubic yards, while the dimensions of concrete work are given on the drawings in feet and inches.

You can save yourself a good many steps in calculating by using fractions to convert the original dimension units into the desired end-result units. Take 1 in., for example. To express 1 in. in feet, you simply put it over 12, thus: 1/12 ft. To express 1 in. in yards, you simply put it over 36, thus: 1/36 yd. In the same manner, to express 1 ft in yards you simply put it over 3, thus: 1/3 yd.

Suppose now that you want to calculate the number of cu yd of concrete in a wall 32 ft long by 14 ft high by 8 in. thick. You can express all these in yards and set up your problem thus:

$$\frac{32}{3} \times \frac{14}{3} \times \frac{8}{36}$$

Next you can cancel out, thus:

$$\frac{\cancel{32}^{16}}{3} \times \frac{\cancel{14}}{3} \times \frac{8}{\cancel{36}_{\cancel{18}_9}} = \frac{896}{81}$$

Dividing 896 by 81, you get 11.06 cu yds of concrete in the wall.

The right triangle is a triangle which contains one right (90°) angle. The following letters will denote the parts of the triangle indicated in figure 2-13—a = altitude, b = base, c = hypotenuse.

In solving a right triangle, the length of any side may be found if the lengths of the other two sides are given. The combinations of 3-4-5 (lengths of sides) or any multiple of these combinations will come out to a whole number. The following examples show the formula for finding

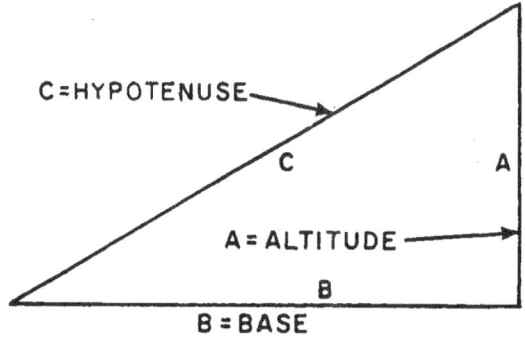

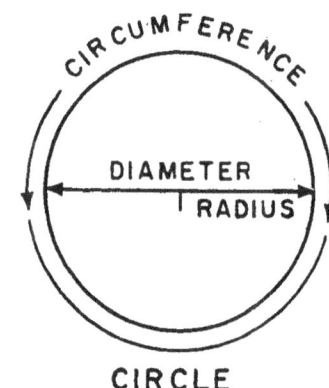

Figure 13.—Right triangle and circle.

each side. Each of these formulas is derived from the master formula $c^2 = a^2 + b^2$.

(1) Find c when a = 3, and b = 4.

$$c = \sqrt{a^2 + b^2} = \sqrt{3^2 + 4^2} = \sqrt{9 + 16} = \sqrt{25} = 5$$

(2) Find a when b = 8, and c = 10.

$$a = \sqrt{c^2 - b^2} = \sqrt{10^2 - 8^2} = \sqrt{100 - 64} = \sqrt{36} = 6$$

(3) Find b when a = 9, and c = 15.

$$b = \sqrt{c^2 - a^2} = \sqrt{15^2 - 9^2} = \sqrt{225 - 81} = \sqrt{144} = 12.$$

There are tables from which the square roots of numbers may be found; otherwise, they may be found arithmetically as explained later in this chapter.

Areas And Volumes Of Geometric Figures

This section on areas and volumes of geometric figures will be limited to the most commonly used geometric figures. Reference books, such as Mathematics, Vol. 1, are available for additional information if needed. Areas are expressed in square units and volumes in cubic units.

1. A circle is a plane figure bounded by a curved line every point of which is the same distance from the center.
    a. The curved line is called the circumference.
    b. A straight line drawn from the center to any point on the circumference is called a radius. (r = 1/2 the diameter.)
    c. A straight line drawn from one point of the circumference through the center and terminating on the opposite point of the circumference is called a diameter. (d = 2 times the radius.) See figure 2-13.
    d. The area of a circle is found by the following formulas: $A = \pi r^2$ or $A = .7854 d^2$. (π is pronounced pie = 3.1416 or 3 1/7, .7854 is 1/4 of π.) Example: Find the area of a circle whose radius is 7". $A = \pi r^2 = 3\ 1/7 \times 7^2 = 22/7 \times 49 = 154$ sq in. If you use the second formula you obtain the same results.
    e. The circumference of a circle is found by multiplying π times the diameter or 2 times π times the radius. Example: Find the circumference of a circle whose diameter is 56 inches. $C = \pi d = 3.1415 \times 56 = 175.9296$ inches.

2. The area of a right triangle is equal to one-half the product of the base by the altitude. (Area = 1/2 base x altitude.) Example: Find the area of a triangle whose base is 16" and altitude 6". Solution:

$A = 1/2\ bh = 1/2 \times 16 \times 6 = 48$ sq in.

3. The volume of a cylinder is found by multiplying the area of the base times the height. ($V = 3.1416 \times r^2 \times h$). Example: Find the volume of a cylinder which has a radius of 8 in. and a height of 4 ft. Solution:

$8\ in = \frac{2}{3}$ ft and $\left(\frac{2}{3}\right)2 = \frac{4}{9}$ sq ft.

$V = 3.1416 \times \frac{4}{9} \times 4 = \frac{50.2656}{9} = 5.59$ cu ft.

4. The volume of a rectangular solid equals the length x width x height. ($V = lwh$.) Example: Find the volume of a rectangular solid which has a length of 6 ft, a width of 3 ft, and a height of 2 ft. Solution:

$V = lwh = 6 \times 3 \times 2 = 36$ cu ft.

5. The volume of a cone may be found by multiplying one-third times the area of the base times the height.

$$\left(V = \frac{1}{3} \pi r^2 h\right)$$

Example: Find the volume of a cone when the radius of its base is 2 ft and its height is 9 ft. Solution:

$$\pi = 3.1416, r = 2, 2^2 = 4$$

$V = \frac{1}{3} r^2 h = \frac{1}{3} \times 3.1416 \times 4 \times 9 = 37.70$ cu ft.

Powers And Roots

1. Powers—When we multiply several numbers together, as 2 x 3 x 4 = 24, the numbers 2, 3, and 4 are factors and 24 the product. The operation of raising a number to a power is a special case of multiplication in which the factors are all equal. The power of a number is the number of times the number itself is to be taken as a factor. Example: 2^4 is 16. The second power is called the square of the number, as 3^2. The third power of a number is called the cube of the number, as 5^3. The exponent of a number is a number placed to the right and above a base to show how many times the base is used as a factor. Example:

$4^3 \leftarrow$ exponent =
   $\leftarrow$ base

$4 \times 4 \times 4 = 64$.

2. Roots—To indicate a root, use the sign $\sqrt{\ }$, which is called the radical sign. A small figure, called the index of the root, is placed in the opening of the sign to show which root is to be taken. The square root of a number is one of the two equal factors into which a number is

divided. Example: $\sqrt{81} = \sqrt{9 \times 9} = 9$. The cube root is one of the three equal factors into which a number is divided. Example: $\sqrt[3]{125} = \sqrt[3]{5 \times 5 \times 5} = 5$.

Square Root

1. The square root of any number is that number which, when multiplied by itself, will produce the first number. For example; the square root of 121 is 11 because 11 times 11 equals 121.

2. How to extract the square root arithmetically:

```
                        95.
        √9025      √90'25.

                   : -81

              180 : 925
              +5  : -925

              185 : 000
```

a. Begin at the decimal point and divide the given number into groups of 2 digits each (as far as possible), going from right to left and/or left to right.
b. Find the greatest number (9) whose square is contained in the first or left hand group (90). Square this number (9) and place it under the first pair of digits (90), then subtract.
c. Bring down the next pair of digits (25) and add it to the remainder (9).
d. Multiply the first digit in the root by 20 and use it as a trial divisor (180). This trial divisor (180) will go into the new dividend (925) five times. This number, 5 (second digit in the root), is added back to the trial divisor, obtaining the true divisor (185).
e. The true divisor (185) is multiplied by the second digit (5) and placed under the remainder (925). Subtract and the problem is solved.
f. If there is still a remainder and you want to carry the problem further, add zeros (in pairs) and continue the above process.

Coverage Calculations

You will frequently have occasion to estimate the number of linear feet of boards of a given size, or the number of tiles, asbestos shingles, and the like, required to cover a given area. Let's take the matter of linear feet of boards first.

What you do here is calculate, first, the number of linear feet of board required to cover 1 sq ft. For boards laid edge-to-edge, you base your calculations on the total width of a board. For boards which will lap each other, you base your calculations on the width laid TO THE WEATHER, meaning the total width minus the width of the lap.

Since there are 144 sq in. in a sq ft, linear footage to cover a given area can be calculated as follows. Suppose your boards are to be laid 8 in. to the weather. If you divide 8 in. into 144 sq in., the result (which is 18 in., or 1.5 ft) will be the linear footage required to cover a sq ft. If you have, say, 100 sq ft to cover, the linear footage required will be 100 x 1.5, or 150 ft.

To estimate the number of tiles, asbestos shingles, and the like required to cover a given area, you first calculate the number of units required to cover a sq ft. Suppose, for example, you are dealing with 9 in. x 9 in. asphalt tiles. The area of one of these is 9 in. x 9 in. or 81 sq in. In a sq ft there are 144 sq in. If it takes 1 to cover 81 sq in., how many will it take to cover 144 sq in.? Just set up a proportional equation, as follows.

$$1:81::x:144$$

When you work this out, you will find that it takes 1.77 tiles to cover a sq ft. To find the number of tiles required to cover 100 sq ft, simply multiply by 100. How do you multiply anything by 100? Just move the decimal point 2 places to the right. Consequently, it takes 177 9 x 9 asphalt tiles to cover 100 sq ft of area.

Board Measure

BOARD MEASURE is a method of measuring lumber in which the basic unit is an abstract volume 1 ft long by 1 ft wide by 1 in. thick. This abstract volume or unit is called a BOARD FOOT.

There are several formulas for calculating the number of board feet in a piece of given dimensions. Since lumber dimensions are most frequently indicated by width and thickness in inches and length in feet, the following formula is probably the most practical.

$$\frac{\text{Thickness in in.} \times \text{width in in.} \times \text{length in ft}}{12}$$

= board feet

Suppose you are calculating the number of board feet in a 14-ft length of 2 x 4. Applying the formula, you get:

$$\frac{\overset{1}{\cancel{2}} \times \overset{2}{\cancel{4}} \times 14}{\underset{\underset{3}{\cancel{6}}}{\cancel{12}}} = \frac{28}{3} = 9\ 1/3\ \text{bd ft}$$

The chief practical use of board measure is in cost calculations, since lumber is bought and sold by the board foot. Any lumber less than 1 in. thick is presumed to be 1 in. thick for board measure purposes. Board measure is calculated on the basis of the NOMINAL, not the ACTUAL, dimensions of lumber.

The actual size of a piece of dimension lumber (such as a 2 x 4, for example) is usually less than the nominal size.